Praise for the hardcover edition of DOUBLE DUTY

"Claudia Black's new book is a gold mine. She was one of the major pioneers in raising our consciousness about Adult Children of Alcoholics. Now in DOUBLE DUTY, she presents clear and precise help for Adult Children who also bear the burden of one or more addictions and/or dysfunctional behaviors. This book gives a much needed specificity to my own work. It offers practical, clinically sound ways for learning to combat the double duty many of us have had to bear. I recommend this book unequivocally."

JOHN BRADSHAW

"There are many books available about Adult Children but Claudia's latest work, DOUBLE DUTY, is exceptional and must reading for both the lay and professional public. It provides knowledge, sensitivity, caring, and truth."

SHARON WEGSCHEIDER-CRUSE

"For far too long, many ACOAs have had to translate existing recovery programs to fit their own experiences. Finally, with the publication of DOUBLE DUTY, the permission has been given to move on. DOUBLE DUTY will surely clarify years of confusion for millions. A *must* read."

MARILYN J. MASON
Coauthor of *Facing Shame: Families in Recovery*

Also by Claudia Black
Published by Ballantine Books:

"IT WILL NEVER HAPPEN TO ME!"
"IT'S NEVER TOO LATE TO HAVE A HAPPY
  CHILDHOOD"
DOUBLE DUTY Dual Dynamics Within the Chemically
  Dependent Home

DOUBLE DUTY

Food Addicted

Dual Dynamics Within the Chemically Dependent Home

Claudia Black

BALLANTINE BOOKS · NEW YORK

Grateful acknowledgment is made to the following for permission to reprint previously published material:

ADULT CHILDREN OF ALCOHOLICS: "The Original Laundry List." Reprinted by permission of Tony A., co-author of *The ACOA Experience*.

AL-ANON FAMILY GROUP HEADQUARTERS, INC.: "Al-Anon: Is It for You?" Copyright © 1980 by Al-Anon Family Group Headquarters, Inc. Reprinted by permission of Al-Anon Family Group Headquarters, Inc. The twelve steps and the twelve traditions of Al-Anon are adapted by permission of AA World Services, Inc. Al-Anon's twelve steps are copyright © 1961 by Al-Anon Family Group Headquarters, Inc. Al-Anon's twelve traditions are copyright © 1961 by Al-Anon Family Group Headquarters, Inc. Reprinted here by permission of Al-Anon Family Group Headquarters, Inc.

ALCOHOLICS ANONYMOUS WORLD SERVICES, INC.: The Twelve Steps and Traditions of Alcoholics Anonymous are reprinted by permission of Alcoholics World Services, Inc. Permission to reprint and adapt The Twelve Steps and Traditions does not mean that AA has reviewed or approved the contents of this publication, nor that AA agrees with the views expressed herein. AA is a program of recovery from alcoholism. Use of The Twelve Steps and Traditions in connection with programs which are patterned after AA but which address other problems does not imply otherwise.

THE FREE PRESS: Figure entitled "Alcohol Addiction" from *Alcohol Problems and Alcoholism* by James E. Royce. Copyright © 1981 by The Free Press. Reprinted with permission of The Free Press, a division of Macmillan, Inc.

NATIONAL COUNCIL ON ALCOHOLISM AND DRUG DEPENDENCE, INC.: "Do You Have the Disease of Alcoholism?" reprinted by permission of the National Council on Alcoholism and Drug Dependence, Inc. Preprinted copies are available from NCAAD, 12 West 21st Street, New York, NY 10010

SIMON & SCHUSTER, INC.: "Are You a Food Addict?" from *The Recovery Sourcebook* by Barbara Yoder. Copyright © by Wink Books. Reprinted by permission of Simon & Schuster, Inc.

Library of Congress Catalog Card Number: 90-34167

ISBN 0-345-37629-3

Printed in Canada

First Ballantine Books Mass Market Edition: January 1992

In memory of my brother, Doug,
the inspiration for *Double Duty*

Contents

Preface

Dear Reader:

After each book I have written I am never certain where my professional work and personal growth will take me next. When *It Will Never Happen to Me* was published in 1981, it represented an exploration in uncharted territory—it contributed to the start of something new—the Adult Children of Alcoholics movement.

While there has been a proliferation of books about Young and Adult Children of Alcoholics since that time, it is important to recognize that the Adult Children of Alcoholics movement is still very young. We are only beginning to understand the complexity of the actual trauma within the dysfunctional family systems that so many Adult Children have experienced, and the various ways this has compromised their adulthood.

Over the years thousands of Adult Children have begun their process of self-healing. There have been many wonderful miracles. Yet, as I've watched people moving through their recovery, I've also seen many individuals hit a baffling, impenetrable wall that halted their progress. There seemed to be a missing link or another piece to the puzzle.

A very big piece of what I believe causes such blockage is the experience of double duty. It is through exploring these issues that we will be able to recognize and confront these challenging dynamics and move on to lasting recovery.

One of the key premises of the ACOA recovery process is putting the past behind us. That only occurs when the truth of one's experience is acknowledged. Up to this time in the evolution of the ACOA movement, the stories told—and as a result the issues addressed—have tended to be very generalized. This stage of emphasizing the experiences all ACOAs have in common has been incredibly valuable. However, now that many Adult Children have spent several years in recovery from their ACOA issues, I believe it is time to explore how Adult Children differ from each other. And that difference is what *Double Duty* is all about.

During the past decade I've taught workshops and conducted professional training sessions from Seattle to Kansas City and Boston to Rio de Janeiro, Tokyo, and Garmish, West Germany. One recurring theme has struck a deep chord in me—the problems people have encountered because of what I've come to call "Double Duty/Dual Identity" issues. These are the intensified life experiences of ACOAs who not only have had to contend with the trauma of family alcoholism, but who have also had to defend against an additional powerful dynamic that profoundly affected their lives. The additional struggle might be with incest or physical disability, being gay or lesbian or a person of color. I met Adult Children who'd been physically abused; ACOAs who'd been sexually abused; ACOAs who had eating disorders; ACOAs who were also chemically dependent; ACOAs who'd been raised as the only child in the family nightmare.

The questions such individuals posed in my workshops/trainings all coalesced in the same psychological pool: "How do I address my ACOA issues in light of my eating disorder?" "How long should I be sober before I address my Adult Child issues?" "How do I factor in the impact of my physical disability as I address my ACOA issues?" "How does my sexual orientation affect my Adult Child issues?" "I'm an ACOA and a minority—sometimes I feel different and alone 'in these rooms.' " And the question so many are asking: "Why am I having such a hard time in therapy?"

All of these individuals were experiencing the same things—when they looked in the mirror they saw their identities expressed in two or more ways. And in that recognition—in that process of looking in the mirror and unearthing their own histories—they began to recognize that what was reflected back to them was not one, but two equally powerful dynamics. These had created profoundly disruptive internal messages that they knew had to be recognized and healed before they could make peace with themselves.

I believe that no human being deserves the shame that is often created by these Double Duty/Dual Identity situations. No one deserves to live with the depth of fear, loneliness, deprivation, and isolation found in the lives of the people throughout this book. I believe that we all deserve to have choices in our lives. In *Double Duty* my intention has been to offer validation to the unique life experiences of these Adult Children and, equally important, to offer an explanation for that "wall" so many ACOAs run into during their recovery process.

It is my hope that the life stories in this book will help all Adult Children come to believe that, no matter how traumatic their past experiences, recovery is possible.

By openly exploring their Double Duty/Dual Identity issues, the contributors have displayed not only rare courage and generosity—they have also reached deeply into themselves and discovered yet another level of their own recovery.

It takes a great deal of inner strength to tell others these kinds of stories and to share so openly. The contributors said things they had never previously spoken, written, or shared in any manner. In opening their souls at such a deep level, they ran the gamut of emotions. They cried; they laughed; they became angry; they grew sad. But as they revealed their vulnerability, they also trusted in the process of their recovery.

At the beginning of our work together nearly all the contributors were strangers to me—though not in spirit. Most of them volunteered their stories for the book at workshops or conferences.

I was deeply moved by the contributors sharing with me so intimately. I can remember that some of the life stories I received in the mail were packaged with a note that read, "Handle with Care."

This wise caution is valuable counsel for all who will read this book. Handle yourself—and the lives of those who are sharing with us—with great care and compassion. These Adult Children are revealing some of their most painful memories of events they experienced at ages five, seven, twelve—memories filled with profound feelings of fear, loneliness, and shame that they have carried from childhood into adulthood.

There has been a tendency by some to be critical of

Adult Children for not moving forward more quickly in recovery. My hope is that *Double Duty* will offer validation to those who have not been able to move on because they first needed a clearer perspective from which to examine their lives. I hope that this book will promote both an expanded sense of self for Double Duty/Dual Identity survivors and a greater understanding of the genuine complexity of the Double Duty/Dual Identity issues by families, friends, and therapists.

I hope that *Double Duty* will be another step in the process of recovery for all of us.

I am with you in spirit.

Claudia Black
October 1990

Acknowledgments

I would like to express my gratitude and say thank you, first and foremost, to all the contributors who participated in this project. While only four life stories appear in DOUBLE DUTY: FOOD ADDICTED, the final book, I am also greatly indebted to many other contributors who offered stories that were not included. Each of your individual contributions helped me to better understand the particular Double Duty/Dual Identity issues presented here.

I would also like to thank my friends and colleagues who gave me such thoughtful feedback. Dr. Leslie Drozd, Victoria Danzig, Skip Sauvain, Mary McClellan, Jack Fahey, Anne Marsin.

Barbara Shor, a heartfelt thanks for the final hand polishing of my prose. And, Cheryl Woodruff, my editor—who walked this journey with me.

DOUBLE DUTY

Food Addicted

1

The Challenge of Double Duty/Dual Identity

Out of the seven of us kids, three are alcoholic, two are married to alcoholics, and the other two are just all screwed up.

—*Adult Child*

Adult Children of Alcoholics (ACA or ACOA) is a term that describes an adult person who was raised in a family affected by parental chemical dependency and co-dependence.

The wording is not meant to imply that this adult-age person behaves as a child. It means that within this person there is an inner spirit—an inner child—who has been hurt and who now needs to be recognized, validated, and healed. Inside this Adult Child is an adult-age person who is as emotionally vulnerable as a nine-year-old or a twelve-year-old. I picture the Adult Child as a nine-year-old with thirty-five years of pain or a twelve-year-old with forty-five years of pain.

The phrase *Adult Children* acknowledges that within each of these adult-age individuals there is a child who has difficulty experiencing a healthy life until he (or she) is able to speak the truth about his childhood and free himself from the bondage of his past. Until this recognition and healing of the past occurs, Adult Children are destined to continue reliving old scripts.

The ACOA movement has allowed thousands of people to recover from the pain of their childhoods. It has given them hope and a sense of direction. It has offered them choices about how they will continue to live their lives from now on.

I first used the term *Adult Children of Alcoholics* (*ACA* or *ACOA*) in 1977, in the initial phases of the development of the concept. Since then the phrase and its acronyms have moved through a variety of changes.

Today, when people speak of ACOAs, they're usually referring to Adult Children who were raised in chemically dependent families. Until recently, "alcoholism" is the term that has been most widely used in the field of substance abuse to describe chemically dependent families. However, over the past decade, "chemical dependency" has become a much more commonly used phrase because it covers both alcohol and other drug dependencies. To be even more inclusive, some professionals use the phrase *Adult Children of Addicted Families*.

More and more people are identifying with Adult Children characteristics—whether or not they were raised in alcoholic families. And because so many are also finding answers in the process of recovery used by ACOAs, this concept has expanded even further until it has become "Adult Children of Dysfunctional Families."

How to Recognize the Adult Child

- We become isolated and afraid of other people, especially authority figures.
- We are frightened by anger and any personal criticism.
- We judge ourselves harshly and have low self-esteem.
- We don't act—we react.
- We are dependent personalities who are terrified of abandonment.
- We will do anything to hold on to a relationship. This is the way we avoid feeling the pain of our parents not having been there for us emotionally.
- We become alcoholics, marry them, or do both. Or we find another compulsive personality, such as a workaholic or an overeater, with whom we continue to play out our fear of abandonment.
- We have become addicted to excitement from years of living in the midst of a traumatic and often dangerous family soap opera.
- We live life from the viewpoint of victims or rescuers and are attracted to victims or rescuers in our love, friendship, and career relationships.
- We confuse love with pity and tend to love people whom we can pity and rescue.
- We felt responsible for the problems of our unstable families, and as a result we do not feel entitled to live independent lives now.
- We get guilt feelings if we stand up for ourselves instead of giving in to others.
- We became approval seekers and lost our own identities in the process.
- We have an overdeveloped sense of responsibility to-

ward others, but we rarely consider our responsibility to ourselves.

• We had to deny our feelings in our traumatic childhoods. This estranged us from all our feelings, and we lost our ability to recognize and express them.

This collection of statements is often referred to as the "Laundry List for Adult Children." It exists in many forms and is widely used in Adult Child self-help groups. See appendix 3, for another variation.

Troubled Families

If you identify with many of the issues presented in the laundry list, it is likely that you were raised in a chemically dependent or otherwise dysfunctional family. What is true for Adult Children from addicted families is also true for people from other kinds of troubled families. These family systems are usually affected by denial, rigidity, isolation, and shame. Sometimes Adult Children can identify the primary source of the dysfunction in the family, sometimes not. It isn't as important to know exactly what caused the dysfunction as it is to recognize the messages internalized during your childhood that you are still reenacting today.

The common denominator for those who identify with Adult Child characteristics is a pervading sense of loss. These are people who as children were raised in families where they experienced loss on a chronic basis. That loss may have been due to physical abandonment, emotional abandonment, or both.

Children from alcoholic and other troubled families could also be referred to as "Children of Denial" or "Children of Trauma." As young people they learned to continually deny, minimize, rationalize, and discount their feelings and their experiences. Some learned to lie blatantly to protect themselves or their family image. Others learned simply not to speak up—so the truth was never told.

Living with such chronic loss—at a time in their young lives when they were developing their identity and sense of self-worth—was very traumatic. Too often people forget that we are referring to children of three, seven, eleven, fifteen years of age. The trauma in their lives has been easy to discount because those around them discounted it and also because COAs demonstrate such phenomenal survivorship skills.

For decades the treatment focus of the chemically dependent family was the alcoholic; it was not until the problems of the emotionally dependent spouse or partner of the alcoholic were recognized that the term *co-alcoholic* was coined. Co-alcoholic implied that the partner was also significantly affected by the disease on psychological, mental, social, and even physical levels as a result of being in a close relationship with a chemically dependent person. Because of this, it was believed that these individuals also needed and deserved treatment and a recovery process of their own. The term "co-dependent" soon replaced "co-alcoholic" because alcoholics were increasingly being referred to as "chemically dependent."

Today, co-dependency no longer reflects only those traits exhibited by the spouse or partner of an alcoholic. It also refers to people whose behavior is characterized by the numbing of feelings, by denial, low self-worth, and compulsive behavior. It manifests itself in relationships when you give another person power over your self-esteem. The ACOA movement was the precursor of the co-dependency movement.

At a recent national conference on co-dependency, a group of 1,800 educators agreed upon a definition of the term. Co-dependency was seen as "a pattern of painful dependency on compulsive behaviors and on approval from others in an attempt to find safety, self-worth, and identity." However, although the great majority of Adult Children manifest co-dependency traits, not all co-dependents are ACOAs.

Double Duty is a book for anyone who identifies with being an Adult Child, no matter what the cause of trauma in the family.

The Healthy Family

Some people question whether or not any of us comes from a healthy family. Cartoonist Jennifer Berman brilliantly captures this sentiment in her cartoon that shows a nearly empty auditorium with a large sign in the back reading, "ADULT CHILDREN OF NORMAL PARENTS ANNUAL CONVENTION."

Although it is true that anyone reading the laundry list could identify with some of the statements on it, only those who have been raised with chronic loss are able to identify with most of them. Such individuals actively need to address what their past means—and how it continues to affect them—in order to create greater choice and balance in their present lives.

Still, it is my belief that there are indeed healthy family systems. In fact, it is often recovering Adult Children who are creating those healthy systems today.

All of us can benefit by looking at the behavioral patterns we encountered in our birth families so that we can take responsibility for reshaping our lives differently as adults. One of the greatest gifts of the Adult Children's movement is the energy directed toward understanding and creating the dynamics of a healthy family.

Since many Adult Children often lack an understanding of what is normal or healthy in family life, the following lists may be helpful.

IN A NURTURING FAMILY . . .
- People feel free to talk about inner feelings.
- All feelings are okay.
- The person is more important than performance.
- All subjects are open to discussion.
- Individual differences are accepted.
- Each person is responsible for his/her own actions.
- Respectful criticism is offered along with appropriate consequences for actions.
- There are few "shoulds."
- There are clear, flexible rules.
- The atmosphere is relaxed.
- There is joy.
- Family members face up to and work through stress.
- People have energy.
- People feel loving.
- Growth is celebrated.
- People have high self-worth.
- There is a strong parental coalition.

IN A DYSFUNCTIONAL FAMILY . . .
- People compulsively protect inner feelings.
- Only "certain" feelings are okay.
- Performance is more important than the person.

- There are many taboo subjects, lots of secrets.
- Everyone must conform to the strongest person's ideas and values.
- There is a great deal of control and criticism.
- There is punishment, shaming.
- There are lots of "shoulds."
- The rules are unclear, inconsistent, and rigid.
- The atmosphere is tense.
- There is much anger and fear.
- Stress is avoided and denied.
- People feel tired, hurt, and disappointed.
- Growth is discouraged.
- People have low self-worth.
- Coalitions form across generations.[1]

Alcoholism as a Disease

Some people in recovery have come to an understanding of the disease process of chemical dependency. Yet this concept is confusing to those who may recognize that their parent was dependent on alcohol or other drugs but still perceive that parent as being willful or bad. What parents do as a result of their chemical dependency may be bad, but it is because of the disease process that they have lost the opportunity for choice. I don't know what those parents would have been like had they not been chemically dependent. But I do know that they would have had a greater range of choices about how they handled their parenting and how they expressed those choices.

Alcoholism has been a part of human history since the beginning of recorded time. But to the astonishment of many, it has been barely twenty-five years since it was formally recognized as a disease. Many professionals think of 1956 as the date of recognition for the disease concept, for it was in that year that the American Medical Association (AMA) first endorsed the admission of alcoholics to general hospitals. It was a major step toward formal recognition of alcoholism as a disease, but that did not occur officially until November 26, 1966, when the house of delegates of the AMA, meeting in Houston, Texas, adopted the following resolution:

> Whereas, the American Medical Association of 1966 recognized that alcoholism is a disease that merits the serious concern of all members of health professions; and whereas, alcoholism is recognized as a serious major health problem throughout the land; therefore be it RESOLVED, that the American Medical Association identifies alcoholism as a complex disease and as such recognizes that the medical components are medicine's responsibility. Such recognition is not intended to relieve the alcoholic of moral or legal responsibility, as provided by law, for any acts committed when inebriated; nor does this recognition preclude civil arrest and imprisonment, as provided by the law, for antisocial acts committed when inebriated.

The *Random House Dictionary* defines disease as "a disordered or incorrectly functioning . . . system of the body resulting from the effect of genetic or developmental errors, . . . poisons, . . . [or] toxicity."

Clearly, alcohol and other drugs are poisons to the body. Although not everyone who drinks experiences delirious effects, 8 to 12 percent of our adult population become dependent psychologically and often physically.

Alcohol Addiction: The Progression of the Disease

OCCASIONAL RELIEF DRINKING

CONSTANT RELIEF DRINKING COMMENCES

INCREASE IN
ALCOHOL TOLERANCE
SNEAKING DRINKS

ONSET OF MEMORY BLACKOUTS
(IN SOME PERSONS)

EARLY STAGE

INCREASING DEPENDENCE ON ALCOHOL

URGENCY OF FIRST DRINKS

CONCERN/COMPLAINTS BY FAMILY

AVOID REFERENCE TO DRINKING

FEELINGS OF GUILT

PREOCCUPATION WITH ALCOHOL

MEMORY BLACKOUTS INCREASE
OR BEGIN

DECREASE OF ABILITY TO STOP
DRINKING WHEN OTHERS DO

LOSS OF CONTROL

GRANDIOSE AND AGGRESSIVE
BEHAVIOR OR EXTRAVAGANCE

ALIBIS FOR DRINKING

MIDDLE STAGE

FAMILY MORE WORRIED, ANGRY

PERSISTENT REMORSE

GOES ON WAGON

CHANGE OF PATTERN

EFFORTS TO CONTROL FAIL REPEATEDLY

TELEPHONITIS

TRIES GEOGRAPHICAL ESCAPE

HIDES BOTTLES

PROMISES OR RESOLUTIONS FAIL

LOSS OF OTHER INTERESTS

FURTHER INCREASE IN MEMORY BLACKOUTS

DENIAL

FAMILY AND FRIENDS AVOIDED

UNREASONABLE RESENTMENTS

WORK AND MONEY TROUBLES

TREMORS AND EARLY MORNING DRINKS

NEGLECT OF FOOD

PROTECTS SUPPLY

PHYSICAL
DETORIORATION

DECREASE IN ALCOHOL TOLERANCE

ONSET OF LENGTHY INTOXICATIONS

IMPAIRED
THINKING

LATE STAGE

DRINKING WITH INFERIORS

INDEFINABLE FEARS

OBSSESSION
WITH

UNABLE TO INITIATE ACTION

DRINKING

VAGUE SPIRITUAL DESIRES

ALL ALIBIS EXHAUSTED

ETHICAL

COMPLETE DEFEAT ADMITTED

DETERIORATION

OBSESSIVE DRINKING CONTINUES
IN VICIOUS CIRCLES

Source: James Royce, *Alcohol Problems and Alcoholism*
(New York: Macmillan/Free Press, 1981).

THE ROAD TO RECOVERY

ENLIGHTENED AND INTERESTING WAY
OF LIFE OPENS UP WITH ROAD
AHEAD TO HIGHER LEVELS THAN
EVER BEFORE

FULL APPRECIATION OF
SPIRITUAL VALUES

GROUP THERAPY AND MUTUAL HELP CONTINUE

CONTENTMENT IN SOBRIETY

FIRST STEPS TOWARD
ECONOMIC STABILITY

CONFIDENCE OF EMPLOYERS

INCREASE OF EMOTIONAL CONTROL

APPRECIATION OF REAL VALUES

FACTS FACED WITH COURAGE

REBIRTH OF IDEALS

NEW CIRCLE OF STABLE FRIENDS

NEW INTERESTS DEVELOP

ADJUSTMENTS TO FAMILY NEEDS

FAMILY AND FRIENDS APPRECIATE EFFORTS

DESIRE TO ESCAPE GOES

REALISTIC THINKING

RETURN OF SELF-ESTEEM

REGULAR NOURISHMENT TAKEN

DIMINISHING FEARS OF THE
UNKNOWN FUTURE

APPRECIATION OF POSSIBILITIES
OF NEW WAY OF LIFE

CARE OF PERSONAL APPEARANCE

ONSET OF NEW HOPE

START OF GROUP THERAPY

PHYSICAL OVERHAUL BY DOCTOR

GUILT REDUCTION

RIGHT THINKING BEGINS

SPIRITUAL NEEDS
EXAMINED

MEETS HAPPY SOBER ALCOHOLICS

STOPS TAKING
ALCOHOL

TOLD ADDICTON CAN BE ARRESTED

LEARNS ALCOHOLISM IS AN ILLNESS

HONEST DESIRE FOR HELP

REHABILITATION

Modified from M. M. Glatt

Yet alcoholism is no more a single disease entity than cancer. Many people are confused about alcoholism because there is not one specific pattern of behavior typical to the alcoholic. Alcoholics often differ in their styles of drinking, and the consequences of their drinking vary widely. Some alcoholics drink daily; others drink in episodic patterns; some stay dry for long intervals between binges. Some drink enormous quantities of alcohol; others do not. Some alcoholics drink only beer; some drink only wine; others choose distilled liquor. Many consume a wide variety of alcoholic beverages and possibly other drugs as well. Today, many alcoholics are dual-addicted—that is, they are addicted to alcohol and another drug, such as marijuana, cocaine, or a prescription pill.

Although alcoholism appears very early in the lives of some people, for others it takes years to develop. Some claim to have started drinking alcoholically from their first drink. Many others report drinking for years before crossing over the "invisible line" that separates social drinking from alcoholic drinking.

While there are exceptions and variations to the rule, most alcoholics experience a progression in their disease. The preceding "dip chart," originally published in 1974 by British physician M.M. Glatt, describes the progression of both the active disease and recovery.

As you read the life stories in the chapters that follow, you will see children responding to parents who are in different stages of the disease. Typically, alcoholism is not even identifiable until someone is in at least middle-stage chemical dependency. This means that children live with the insidious effects of the disease long before it is recognized as a real problem. When alcohol or other drug usage does become more recognizable as a key contributor to the problem, denial, misinformation, and stigma have already spread throughout the family system. Family members have learned their adaptive roles and are trying to survive. At this point, many children still don't recognize their parents' chemical dependency in spite of its blatancy because they have learned the rules of all dysfunctional families: 1) Don't talk; 2) Don't feel; 3) Don't trust; 4) Don't think; 5) Don't ask questions. There is also another problem— very often many family members don't understand alcoholism well enough to recognize it when it smacks them in the face.

Not every alcoholic will experience all of the symptoms shown on the chart, nor do the symptoms have to occur in the exact order presented. In addition, the disease's rate of progression varies. Alcoholism tends to be more rapid for some individuals in some races, which is probably the result of a physiological predisposition. Generally, the progression of the disease is faster for women and young alcoholics than for men. Some alcoholics take thirty or forty years to reach the "chronic" late stage. Others remain in the middle stage indefinitely. However, my clinical experience has demonstrated that Children of Alcoholics who have problems with alcohol move through the progression much more quickly than those with alcohol problems which are not biologically related.

Children within the family may be affected differently. One reason for the variance is birth order. As each child is born, he or she enters the family life story at a different point in the progression of the disease. Should they enter the family prior to the onset of chemical dependency or in the earlier stages of the disease, they are more likely to have had attention focused on them as individual children rather than merely as objects, and they would have experienced greater stability and predictable adult behavior in their earlier years. This frequently creates a greater internal sense of security than that experienced by siblings who enter the family drama at a later point.

But we must recognize that children are not affected only by the chemically dependent parent. They are equally affected by the entire family system, which includes the nonchemically dependent parent (if there is one). Most typically, as the chemically dependent partner moves through the disease progression, the nonaddicted spouse will become more and more preoccupied with the partner's drinking and what that person is thinking and doing. The spouse often begins to display "enabling" behavior to the alcoholic by learning to deny what is going on. Also, the spouse keeps trying to control the alcoholic's behavior, often without understanding what is actually happening.

As the disease progresses, the co-dependent mate becomes angry and depressed and often seeks forms of escape to handle his or her own escalating confusion, guilt, and helplessness. It is no surprise that the children often get left behind in the shuffle and end up living without the focus and attention they need. Their lives are distorted by the unrealistic expectations, unpredictability, rigid (or total lack of) discipline, chaos, tense silence, and abuse from both the alcoholic and the co-dependent parent.

Effects of Family Roles

Children in chemically dependent families do whatever they can to withstand the losses they are experiencing in the family environment. Surprisingly, most children from troubled families have the ability to "look good" to outsiders despite what may be happening in the home. Unfortunately, for the most part looking good is based on survivorship and denial. Children accommodate themselves to whatever environment they are being raised in. They keep trying to bring consistency, structure, and safety into a household that is unpredictable, chaotic, and frightening. To do this they adopt certain roles, or a mixture of these roles, in the family. My research indicates that 60 percent of COAs identify themselves as the *overly responsible* (hero) child; 63 percent identify themselves as the family *placater*; 40 percent identify with being the *adjuster* (lost child); and 20 percent identify with being the *acting-out* child (scapegoat).[2] As the statistics indicate, most people identify with more than one role or recognize that at certain times their roles switch. Many people from other types of troubled families identify with those roles as well.

THE RESPONSIBLE CHILD

This is the child who takes responsibility for whatever is tangible in the environment—people, places, and things. This is the child who sets the table, puts dinner on the table, and sees to it that the children are all sitting down with the right expressions on their faces before the alcoholic parent gets to the table. This is the child known as the "little adult," or the "household top sergeant."

Responsible children become their own parent, a parent to their siblings, and a parent to the parents. It is extremely difficult for these children to be perceived as being in any emotional trouble because, externally, they look very good. They often become the face for the chemically dependent home. Their appearance says to themselves and to the community that everything is just fine here, things are under control.

CORE EMOTIONS:
Fear
Loneliness
Hurt
Powerlessness
Anger
Sadness
Embarrassment

STRENGTHS:
Organized
Goal-oriented
Self-disciplined
Leadership ability
Willingness to take charge
Decisive

DEFICITS:
Difficulty with listening
Difficulty with following
Difficulty with negotiating
Difficulty with asking for help, input, or advice
Difficulty playing
Perfectionist behavior

EMOTIONALLY:
Serious
Rigidly removed from feelings
Perceives experiencing feelings as a loss of control

THE ADJUSTER

This is the child who doesn't want to be emotionally or socially invested in what is occurring in the family. These children shrug their shoulders and say, "It doesn't bother me. I don't care."

Adjusters spend their time trying to be less visible and, as a result, don't draw much attention to themselves—negative or positive. An adjuster is often referred to as the "lost child." These children also don't have the ability to cry out for help or to say there is something wrong in their lives. They take the stance of, "I can handle it. I'm tough. I can adjust. If I am not invested, then I am not going to get hurt. Just don't think about it. "

STRENGTHS:
Flexibility
Ability to adjust
Easygoing attitude and personality
Not willing to be preoccupied with negativity

DEFICITS:
Inability to lead
Inability to initiate
Fearful of making decisions
Inability to see options
Reacts without thinking

EMOTIONALLY:
Aloof

Withdrawn, or can be pleasant as a defense mechanism

THE PLACATER

This is the "household social worker," the child who takes responsibility for the emotional well-being of all the family members. This child takes on the task of reducing and minimizing the expressed and sometimes unexpressed fears, sadness, anger, and embarrassment of the whole family. Placaters are warm, caring, empathetic young people. Again, they are expert at not drawing attention to themselves as children in need.

STRENGTHS:
Warm
Caring
Empathetic
Good listener
Nice smile
Ability to give
Sensitive to others

DEFICITS:
Difficulty with receiving
Inability to focus on self
Incredible guilt for self-focus
Highly tolerant of inappropriate behavior
Highly fearful of mistakes

EMOTIONALLY:
Extremely warm and interested in others

Closed to their own feelings of inadequacy, fear, and
sadness

THE ACTING-OUT CHILD

This is the one who is willing to scream to the world
that there is something wrong here. Unfortunately, even
when this child does so, the alcoholism may still not
get identified or addressed. This child challenges authority more blatantly than the others and, as a result, is more likely to be in trouble in school and in
the community. In reality, acting-out children tend
to suffer less from denial than the others in the chemically dependent family. They are closer to knowing
the truth and are acting out the dysfunction of the
family.

STRENGTHS:
Good leadership ability, recognizing they just lead in
    the wrong direction
Less denial, closer to the truth
Less apt to subscribe to the "Don't talk" rule
Creative

DEFICITS:
Hurtful expression of anger
Greater lack of social skills
Intrusive with others
Greater difficulty entering the mainstream of life due
    to tendency to challenge authority and unwillingness
    to follow directions

EMOTIONALLY:
Angry
Most fearful of their sadness and their fears

Acting-out children, more than the other role players, are more likely to enter into an addictive process at a younger age. If their addiction is chemical dependency, they will progress through the stages of their drug/ alcohol dependency at a younger age. Consequently they may also die earlier from those dependencies—or get well sooner.

Whether these role players are drawing positive or negative attention to themselves, or being invisible, all of these ACOAs are learning such rules as:

Don't talk honestly.
Don't express your feelings.
Your feelings don't count.
You are not important.
You can't trust anybody.
No one will be there for you.
Your perceptions aren't accurate.
There is no time to play.
Other people's needs are more important than your own.

These roles typify the experiences of children who have lived with great loneliness, fear, sadness, disappointment, anger, guilt, and shame. They are COAs who have lived and struggled with powerlessness. The roles they have adopted are the ways they learned to mask their chronic losses and their different methods of coping with their feelings.

The Adult Child and Progression

It is important to understand that what has been seeded in a dysfunctional childhood takes a grave toll in dramatic ways in adulthood. And it is in adulthood that these problems finally begin to surface. There are many symptoms:

- Depression
- Inability to develop or maintain a healthy relationship
- Remaining victimized within a destructive relationship
- Poor parenting skills
- Inability to actualize one's potential or talent, inability to experience accomplishments in spite of proven abilities
- Compulsive behaviors
- Addictions

The problems of Adult Children are rarely identified until the individuals are at least in their late twenties or early thirties. When seventeen-, eighteen-, and nineteen-year-old Adult Children begin to leave their families of origin, there is usually no time for quiet self-reflection. At this point many ACOAs hold on to their survivorship skills for dear life and, as many put it, "move on," not thinking, not feeling, not talking about their growing-up years. Yet they usually continue to stay emotionally enmeshed with their families.

It is not until ACOAs begin to experience more of a normal daily routine in their lives that these issues become increasingly visible to themselves and possibly others. As with alcoholism, Adult Child issues escalate over time. But these problems don't tend to hit like a dramatic bolt of lightning. Adult Children are often deep in the throes of a troubling situation before they recognize that there is a problem.

Not recognizing a problem until it reaches the crisis

stage is one of the core issues of ACOAs. This is because they have spent years learning to dismiss relevant cues and signals in order to survive. Such a capacity for denial can create an endless loop in which ACOAs are forever reacting to problems.

Another Adult Child issue that interferes with the process of seeking help is that, as young people, they learned that it was not safe or okay to ask for help. They came to believe that no one would be there for them if they did.

When we add up these three dynamics—that problems enter and escalate in our lives slowly; that we don't recognize a problem until it has reached the crisis stage; and that we don't trust the process of asking for help—we can begin to understand why it may have taken us such a long time to be able to address these issues.

Another significant factor in recovery for Adult Children is that, until the ACOA movement began, information about these problems and their solutions wasn't available. Our understanding of these dynamics did not begin until the late 1970s, and recovery resources have only been widely available since the mid-1980s.

It is very common for ACOAs to berate themselves for being so "old" before they began to recognize that they were Adult Children and see how it has affected their lives. Please remember that it doesn't matter how old you are when you begin your recovery. What matters is that you are here now and ready to begin this work. Recovery is possible for anyone at any age. To date, my oldest Adult Child was eighty-six, and most recently I met a woman who had just begun her Adult Child recovery at an enthusiastic seventy-five.

Beyond Survivorship

Denial has been a powerful part of every ACOA's life. If you've allowed yourself even a few thoughts about your dysfunctional or troubled family, you might at first have seen only your strengths. Adult Children are incredible survivors! As a youngster some of the strengths you learned were:

To take charge, to lead
To make adult decisions
To be self-reliant
To be autonomous
To solve problems creatively
To be a hard worker
To be loyal
To develop empathic skills
To develop your talents in art, writing, music, and so on, to provide a safe escape
To respond effectively in a crisis.

The list could go on and on.

We certainly deserve to feel good about our strengths however they were developed. Yet by ignoring what it was we didn't learn, our lives remain very limited. It is by acknowledging what didn't get learned in our childhood, as well as discovering what we learned that is no longer useful, that Adult Children can establish a direction for recovery.

Adult Children need to explore their pasts, and in doing so, they need to identify the helpful and the hurtful aspects of their growing-up years. The skills that were helpful in the past, and that remain helpful today, can certainly support you in your recovery. However, that which is hurtful must be stopped and new behavior learned in its place.

For example, learning self-reliance may have been most helpful as a child. However, as an adult you may be self-reliant to the point where you totally exclude others, which leaves you feeling lonely and isolated. Moving out of the perception that only extremes are valid will allow you to maintain a healthy self-reliance while simultaneously learning how to become interdependent with others. Recovery means that you will now have the opportunity to make conscious decisions in your life.

People in recovery are highly critical of what they refer to as their co-dependent behavior when they were children and adolescents. We must remember that these were survival skills. I don't think it was possible for us to behave any differently under the circumstances at that time in our lives. Don't be critical of your survivor self. Be accepting of your courage and vulnerability under difficult circumstances. The key to healthy living in adulthood is to recognize when we are maintaining survival skills that no longer work for us. We need to let go of old behavior that interferes with enjoying the type of life we would like to live now. Remember, childhood survivor skills carried into adulthood can continue to maintain a co-dependent life-style.

Many Adult Children are hesitant about beginning their recovery because they don't want to blame their parents for what they see as their own adult problems. *Recovery is not a blaming process.* Rather, it is a process of examining and speaking your truths. It is the process of breaking your denial, of acknowledging and taking ownership of your feelings and your life. In doing so, you may need to acknowledge pain from childhood and to be specific about where that pain came from. However, the goal is not to blame, but to be able to break the rules that have kept you in denial and disengaged from your self. Adult Children are fiercely loyal and are often frightened of betraying their families. But if there is any betrayal here, it is of the chemical addiction and co-dependency. You aren't betraying those parts of your mother and father that loved you. I believe our parents truly want us to be healthy and happy, but often their afflictions have gotten in the way. The only true act of betrayal is when we betray ourselves by not speaking our own truth.

Resources for Recovery

Some people began working on their ACOA issues before the concept of Adult Children came into being. Special focus groups for the Adult Child did not begin to develop until the late 1970s. Until that time, when people did seek help, many could not identify themselves as "Adult Children." Although some individuals were able to resolve issues related to their childhood without this label, most people ignored the primary issues.

In 1976 and 1977, when I began my work with Adult Children in southern California, Stephanie Brown was also addressing the issues at the Stanford Alcohol Clinic; and Sharon Wegscheider-Cruse, then in Minneapolis, was spreading the word about family alcoholism. In the late seventies in New York City a small group of Twelve Step Al-Anon members met at the Smithers Institute to form a new group called Hope for Adult Children of Alcoholics. This first formal meeting was also held under the auspices of Al-Anon.

At that time one of the members of this group, Tony A., developed the original "laundry list" of Adult Child symptoms (see appendix 3). This list has become a mainstay for ACOA self-help groups throughout the country. Over the next few years there was some confusion about unapproved literature at meetings and whether or not Adult Children needed to organize separate Al-Anon meetings for themselves. As a result of such concerns, there are a few hundred Al-Anon-affiliated Adult Child groups nationwide, while several hundred other Twelve Step groups for Adult Children exist that are not affiliated with Al-Anon.

TWELVE STEP GROUPS

You will see that many of the people in this book have sought recovery through the use of various Twelve Step programs, such as ACA Al-Anon, ACA/ACOA, non–Al-Anon ACA/ACOA, traditional Al-Anon, Overeaters Anonymous (OA), Cocaine Anonymous (CA), Narcotics Anonymous (NA), and others. These groups were spawned as an outgrowth of the oldest, largest ongoing self-help Twelve Step program in the world—Alcoholics Anonymous (AA). The groups that have followed in the path of AA, which began in 1935, have developed a spiritual self-help program based on AA's Twelve Steps and Twelve Traditions.

The self-help groups familiar to most Adult Children of Alcoholics are AA, ACA/ACOA Anonymous, ACA AlAnon, Al-Anon, Co-Dependents Anonymous (CODA). These particular groups are organized around Twelve Step meetings. They usually last an hour to an hour and a half (depending on the region of the country). They adhere to the leaderless group model and follow a similar format, with a different person directing the meetings each time. The group usually begins with a reading of the laundry list and the Twelve Steps, and this is followed by a qualifying discussion or a discussion of a selected topic chosen from the program literature.

In these meetings people speak from their own experiences. They talk about whatever is on their minds as it relates to addiction and recovery or to unhealthy behavior they have identified in themselves and are beginning to change. There is no cross talk—which means that no one is allowed to give advice or direct another person's process. No one is required to share. There are no dues or fees.

Twelve Step and other self-help groups offer people an opportunity to realize that their experiences and feelings are not unique, but that in fact their problems are very similar to those each group member has experienced at some time.

Another unifying aspect of recovery support groups is that they practice the rule of anonymity. Who you are by name is not what is important, and as a rule, last names are not used. As well, the information shared in the meeting is not to be disclosed outside the room. In this way no matter what your financial or social status, you are considered equal to all human beings who suffer from the same issues as yourself. Each participant is helped through the support and understanding of the group.

ACOA groups offer a simple program with guidelines for understanding your situation and suggested steps to help you develop and sustain the new strengths and capabilities needed to counteract the old internalized messages of your dysfunctional past. These groups also

provide opportunities for social interaction and feedback from recovering peers.

Some Adult Children have also found resources
through self-help groups that are not Twelve Step–
oriented. Often such alternatives may simply be a group
of Adult Children who choose to get together and develop their own support network.

THERAPY AS A RESOURCE

My theory is that ACOAs who are addressing Double
Duty/Dual Identity issues—where difficulty in trusting
others is often primary—are most likely to feel safer in
the one-to-one therapy process before they feel ready
for a group. Many Double Duty/Dual Identity people
may need individual therapy before they can effectively
use group therapy, or they may find that using both
simultaneously proves to be the most beneficial.

Many Adult Children like and benefit from the group
model but prefer it to be led by a counselor, educator,
or therapist. Educators and clinicians have readily responded to information and a model of treatment that
is proving to be particularly helpful to Adult Children.
Adult Children often begin their work with an educational, time-limited support group with a small number
of other Adult Children led by a therapist. Such groups
are usually highly structured in terms of their content
and will be limited to a certain number of meetings.
People often move into long-term group therapy after
participating in such educational groups or individual
therapy.

Each of us is an individual, and each of us is in a
different place in our recovery. While some Adult Children choose to work on their issues in a more isolated
fashion through reading, others are using support groups

offered by their churches. Most people use a combination of resources, including different self-help groups, reading, pastoral and psychological counseling, and individual and group therapy. Above all, what is important is to choose a path of recovery that is right for you, that is safe, and that offers you exactly what you want.

It is also my hope that the counselors and therapists reading this book will recognize that, because different ACOAs experience the same issues with differing intensities, it is important to develop a greater respect for individual pacing in the therapeutic process. We may not necessarily be able to use the same treatment plan for each Adult Child. We need to start where the client is.

The Growth of the ACOA Movement

ACOA is a very young movement—one that developed from the grass-roots level. However, it commanded a great deal of media attention. In a very short period of time—approximately ten years—thousands of Adult Children self-help groups have been created, and hundreds of books are now available on the subject. Many therapists are now targeting their practices to serve this special client population. Elementary schools and high schools are developing support groups for young COAs. National advocacy groups such as the National Association for Children of Alcoholics are developing and offering resources. The concept of co-dependency, although not limited to ACOAs, has also emerged as an accepted phenomenon, and it too has created its own proliferation of books, organizations, and attention.

Conferences for ACOAs are now being routinely held in every city in the nation, and these command large audiences. Entertainers and famous athletes are speaking out about their personal experiences as ACOAs. Publishers in other countries are rapidly translating books on these topics so that recovery support will soon be available worldwide—from Japan to India, and from Germany to Uruguay.

Of course, as with any movement that seizes the imagination of so many, the ACOA movement has generated enough energy to create a strong counterreaction. There are individuals who genuinely believe that it is only a fad. There are individuals who say the ACOA movement is self-serving for a small group of professionals, or that it is the "yuppie disease," meaning that it isn't relevant to a mainstream population and therefore has no value. Some say it is composed of adults who want to blame others and not take responsibility for their own lives. The objections go on and on.

The loudest critics appear to be those who are often the most uninformed or misinformed. These individuals revel in taking a single word of knowledge and transforming it into a volume of misinformation. They are often very frightened and quite possibly in denial themselves. Often they are individuals who have not been willing to open up to their own vulnerabilities.

Yet, as in any movement, there are aspects that can be hurtful. There may be people who take advantage of the movement or who take advantage of Adult Children by attempting to simplify serious issues that need to be addressed in great depth. But throwing the baby out with the bathwater serves no purpose. Valid criticism does not invalidate the importance and the value of this movement.

There are people who have spent years in therapy who are still unable to address their core issues because their family-of-origin issues were discounted or ignored. There are thousands of people within our communities who are the "walking wounded" because their ACOA issues have not been recognized or addressed. Their pain, which has both a legitimate basis and the potential for resolution, was not allowed to emerge. These people were encouraged to discount their feelings and keep them hidden.

That denial does not have to continue. Today there are hundreds of thousands of people from all walks of life—from prisons and psychiatric facilities to schoolrooms and corporate boardrooms—who are benefiting from what we have learned about Adult Children and the process of recovery. Today, Adult Children can heal, learn to make choices, and accept responsibility for how they live their lives.

The ACOA movement developed because so many Adult Children have begun to recognize what they have in common with each other. For the first time in their lives they no longer feel alone and isolated. They no longer feel as if there is something inherently wrong with who they are. They understand that there are reasons for how they have lived their lives. Guilt, shame, loneliness, and fear have been lessened. Hope and joy have become a genuine part of lives once dominated by pain.

Adult Children are learning basic skills, such as identifying and expressing feelings, problem-solving, establishing boundaries, setting limits. They are learning to trust and find healthy ways to include others in their lives. As a result of this collective effort, resources such as self-help groups specifically oriented toward Adult Children and private therapy groups for Adult Children are now available nationwide.

Double Duty/Dual Identity

I have observed many Adult Children belittling and crit-
icizing themselves for not moving through recovery as
easily or as speedily as others they know. I have found
that when ACOAs are unable to work through the process with as much ease or speed as they would like, it
is often because of their need to identify and address
multiple issues in recovery. People who have multiple
issues often have an additional need to protect themselves, and this may be why they do not connect with
self-help groups or the group therapy process as quickly
as others.

This book describes in detail the process the child
experiences in an alcoholic family. It also examines the
special problems of multiple issues—which I call
"Double Duty/Dual Identity" (DD/DI)—that these
Adult Children face, and the step-by-step process of
their recovery. We can no longer continue to apply ge-
neric recovery programs to all ACOAs. While general
recovery information is most often what one needs to
focus on in early recovery, in time an individual's unique
life situation has to be and deserves to be addressed.
By refusing to look at the specifics of an individual's
experiences we can inadvertently trivialize the purpose
of the entire movement.

The concept of Double Duty is not meant to encour-
age people to use their differentness to keep others away
or to resist new opportunities. I believe we must first
see our commonalities, and humble and comfort ourselves in the realization that we are not unique. Although we suffered separately, we have not suffered
alone. Only after we have acknowledged this common

ground should we take the time to explore what may have been unique to our experiences.

There are many reasons for differences among Adult Children. Birth order affects children differently, sex role expectations affect children differently. Who the chemically dependent parent is, and the dynamics of how co-dependency shows itself, create differences among ACOAs. While many areas merit exploration, In my research I have chosen to focus on nine specific *Double Duty* issues that offer a conceptual framework on which others may build.

Double Duty exists when a child has one major trauma-inducing dynamic in the family and there exists an additional dynamic that reinforces the consequences through added trauma or complexity. Sometimes the additional dynamic may be physical abuse; other times it might be a life circumstance such as being an only child. (Being an only child in and of itself doesn't have to lead to trauma; in fact, it can have many advantages. But in the context of an alcoholic or troubled family, being an only child is a major disadvantage.)

I envision the Double Duty COA as a small child, hunched over, dragging unwieldy boxes and overflowing bags of trauma, when suddenly a dump truck comes roaring up and adds another load of pain.

For instance, if there is a terminally ill sibling in a child's family, growing up can be quite traumatic. But it does not have to create lifelong trauma if there is a healthy family system to help the surviving child respond to the situation. However, put the same set of circumstances in an alcoholic or otherwise troubled family, and the child involved will suffer many long-lasting effects from both issues. This is what I mean by a Double Duty situation.

In order to endure such trauma and added complexity—simply in order to survive—this child has to toughen up much more than other children. In adulthood, such survivors are likely to have their defenses rigidly in place and their emotions very hardened.

By contrast, Dual Identity is a special form of Double Duty in which one has at least two equally commanding aspects to one's identity—such as being a COA and a person of color, or being a COA and gay or lesbian. It is like looking into a two-sided mirror and seeing one image of yourself on one side and an equally real but different image on the other side. Although the images are different, they are invisibly enmeshed. This leaves Adult Children even more confused about who they are and what is most important in their lives.

For an Adult Child to experience a full recovery it is important to recognize that, as an ACOA, there may be other, equally significant aspects of your identity that need to be recognized and addressed—beyond those of having been raised in a chemically dependent family.

Double Duty/Dual Identity are examples of the synergistic effect of multiple-core issues that many Adult Children experience. The added dynamics of Double Duty/Dual Identity often force children to protect themselves even further. As a result, issues such as not trusting, not feeling, fear of losing control, and an overwhelming sense of shame are experienced even more deeply. It then becomes much more difficult for the afflicted ACOA to ask for help or to feel any hope. Very often the feeling of being overwhelmed by emotion or of having frozen emotions greatly impedes the ability to connect with a recovery process.

There are many people who know they are Adult Children, who know resources are available, who may even truly want to change their lives—yet always find that something seems to get in the way when they try to connect with a helping resource or try to stay involved once they've found that resource. There are others who are so powerfully defended against their pain that their level of denial is too strong for them even to recognize that their lives could be better. Still others become stuck in the process of recovery and "spin their wheels." These are often the DD/DI people.

While there are many life experiences that might merit the Double Duty or Dual Identity label, I have chosen to examine food addictions in this particular book. I have by no means meant to discount other Double Duty/Dual Identity situations. In fact, it is my hope that the life stories included in this volume will offer validation not only to those who recognize aspects of themselves in the lives presented here, but to those who experience Double Duty/Dual Identity situations that we have not addressed.

FOOD ADDICTIONS

Dual Identity is a special case of Double Duty. It describes the aspects of one's identity that, when coupled with being raised in a chemically dependent family, create two distinct yet invisibly enmeshed selves. Food addictions and chemical addictions differ from other Dual Identities in that they are the direct consequences of living with substance abuse. They also represent the two most predominant addictions for Adult Children. It is important for all Adult Children in recovery from substance addictions to examine carefully the interplay between both identities.

The majority of people with food addictions begin that pattern of compromise in childhood. Food offers solace and comfort. It becomes a friend to an already lonely child. Eating, purging, or starving may be a way to exhibit some control in a life that is out of control. But it may also offer a punishment for feelings of inadequacy. In addition, eating can represent one's defiance of powerlessness. The COA's relationship with food often becomes disturbed and takes on meaning beyond the sustenance it was meant to provide.

The contributors in DOUBLE DUTY: FOOD ADDICTED have demonstrated a lot of courage and strength in their lives. By speaking of their lives and recovery, others raised in chemically dependent families may have an opportunity to deal with their silence, too. It is my hope that this book will offer a greater validation and understanding of these life experiences. More importantly, I hope it will offer both inspiration and a path for recovery.

Notes

1. Found through ACOA Self-Help Literature. Original source unknown.
2. C. Black, S. Bucky, S. Padilla, "The Interpersonal and Emotional Consequences of Being an Adult Child of an Alcoholic," *Journal of International Addictions* 21 (May 1986); 213–32.

Life
Stories

How to Use This Book

In *Double Duty: Food Addicted*, I have illustrated the issues of a particular Double Duty group through the truth of their life stories. The participants are in many different phases of recovery and have used different resources in the recovery process.

For the purposes of anonymity, all names have been changed. Portions of stories have been altered to provide even further anonymity. Any resemblance to your life, or to the life of someone you know, is coincidental and most likely due to the myriad commonalities in alcoholic and troubled families.

In many of these stories you might find yourself wishing for additional information or wondering what happened next. Please recognize that the gaps that appear in the stories may reflect gaps in the memories of the contributors themselves. Some contributors chose not to share aspects of their lives to protect anonymity and to maintain personal boundaries. Moreover, the purpose of this book is to explore Double Duty/Dual Identity issues. In order to maintain this focus, it was not possible to offer a more extensive description of each contributor's life.

It is very easy to identify with many of the Double Duty/Dual Identity variables in this book. My advice is to try not to become overwhelmed or preoccupied with the number of additional dynamics that have operated in your life. It is much more important to focus on acknowledging that there are legitimate reasons why you experience your life as you do. Coming from a Double Duty or Dual Identity background is one of those reasons. Always remember: You are not crazy. You are not at fault. Owning this will move you through recovery with a greater acceptance of yourself—one that will ultimately support a deeper level of healing.

Obviously *Double Duty: Food Addicted* is a very serious book, and I pray that it is an equally sensitive book. As you read, think ahead to how you can best take care of yourself if you find you are feeling vulnerable, angry, or sad.

Who knows you are reading this book? Do you have someone trustworthy to talk with if the going gets rough? I believe it is very important to share your feelings with another Adult Child or a counselor or therapist at this time. You will undoubtedly be experiencing feelings and memories of experiences from your past that you never realized had significance, and the intensity of these emotions must not be denied.

Keeping a Journal. As you become immersed in the life stories of the contributors, you may find that keeping a journal can be extremely helpful in your own recovery work. You may want to underline or highlight the statements or themes in *Double Duty* that you find especially meaningful and relevant to your own life. Then use your journal to record your own personal history, memories, flashes of insight, and questions for further thought that emerge as a result of reading that particular passage in the book.

You may want to begin the journal work each time by first writing down the date. This will help you keep track of your own inner journey by following the trail of insights as they occur one by one. Next, you might transcribe the passage in the book (noting the page number) that is triggering your response.

Then, just let your process flow as it will. Simply write down whatever thought first pops into your head, and the next thought, and the next. Try not to be critical of what you're writing or how you're writing it—that makes no difference. What is important is what you are saying to yourself.

Just let the flow continue until you have nothing more to say at that point. Then, either continue reading the book or, if you find yourself fatigued, just stop for the day. Return to the reading and journaling process whenever it feels right to you. If you find passages in the book too painful to read, try not to be frightened by your feelings. Simply remind yourself that it is critical that you be truly aware of how personal the story you are reading has become for you.

You might want to wait a few days to read what you've written in your journal. You may find yourself surprised by what you've written and the depth of your own wisdom. New insights may be triggered by rereading your journal from time to time as you're working through *Double Duty.* You might also find it helpful to share some of your journal entries with your therapist. But keeping a journal is like having a private rendezvous with yourself—you may not wish to share it with anyone, and you don't have to.

Final Considerations. This book was never meant to be read quickly—certainly not in one sitting. Read it slowly. And read it with the support of people who love you and who understand the nature of the issues you may be struggling with.

2

Eating Disorders

*What I learned from growing up in an alcoholic family
was that the world was a painful and scary place. Food
became my means of escaping from those feelings.*

— Adult Child

C ompulsive overeating, bulimia, and anorexia are
all aspects of the same disease—food dependency. Compulsion, obsession, and denial are
the common denominators that weave through these dependencies.

Most people who are compulsive overeaters are not
obese. They are much more likely to be chronically ten
to twenty pounds overweight and preoccupied compulsively with food and body size. Compulsive overeaters
react to sugars and starches in extreme ways. They experience mood changes ranging from euphoric highs to
irritability, from feeling nurtured and comforted to being in a mental frenzy or stupor.

The most visible eating disorder is overeating that
results in obesity. Although this chapter discusses the
psychological factors that influence extreme overeating

43

and create obesity, it must be remembered that under some circumstances, obesity can be caused by purely physiological conditions. There are rare metabolic exceptions and genetic considerations that create obesity. Nonetheless, whatever the reasons for obesity, the psychological, social, and physical consequences are severe. It has been well established that obese people have shorter life spans due to strokes, heart attacks, and arteriosclerosis.

Bulimia is a second form of eating disorder. Bulimics overeat, typically in binges, and then they purge through laxative use, diuretic (water pills) abuse, or by forced vomiting and compulsive exercise. Bulimics, like most compulsive overeaters, tend to be within ten to twenty pounds of average weight. The binge and purge cycle of bulimia closely parallels the highs and crashes that drug addicts know so well. First comes the euphoric high of the binge, then comes the drastic expulsion of the food.

Anorexia is a third type of eating disorder. Anorexics, however, are obsessed with *not* eating. They may even have an unnatural fear of food. Anorexics starve themselves—a compulsion that is often reinforced by the biological euphoria produced by starvation.

Starving and bingeing/purging can produce serious medical problems ranging from dehydration and disturbances in the body's fluid and mineral balance to irreversible liver damage, diabetes, hypoglycemia, heart attacks, and kidney failure. In some cases, gorging and forced vomiting rupture the stomach or esophagus, causing infections and death.

Whatever the form of the disorder, eating takes on a compulsive quality. People feel driven to eat or to starve as though they had no choice. This compulsion effectively blocks awareness of their feelings and serves to distract them from anxiety and from unpleasant feelings and memories. When people are frightened of their feelings, or experience painful feelings, excessive food intake or extreme food deprivation helps them deny and repress the pain.

Overeaters also indulge in food when they're happy and joyful. Many overeat as a reward. Food can become the answer to any feeling.

People who feel poorly about themselves often use food for solace. Those with low self-esteem and a tendency to isolate themselves are much more likely to regard food as a friend. Food nurtures. Food anesthetizes.

People who are overburdened with shame, who have come to believe they are defective or bad, often find that compulsive overeating is the best way to assuage this pain. However, it can also be a form of self-punishment—a consciously abusive act. Overeating fuels the bulimic's sense of shame, while purging is sometimes an attempt to alleviate even greater shame. The anorexic may unconsciously be looking for a way to become invisible, to disappear.

Bulimics and anorexics often feel revulsion about their bodies and starve or purge themselves as punishment. This revulsion may be fed by a distorted perception of their bodies. They often see themselves as fat when they are quite thin or of average body weight. Overeaters may be repulsed by their bodies and overeat in response to their feelings of futility and powerlessness. Yet overeaters usually have distorted perceptions, too. Most often they believe they're smaller than they actually are, yet some see themselves as larger than they are. Early on, they all quit looking in the mirror. And they all tend to be disconnected from their bodies.

Both overeaters and undereaters have a great deal of difficulty verbalizing their internal experiences. This is because they're removed from both their feelings and their needs. They don't recognize the internal and external cues and signals that serve as indicators of their true needs.

People with eating disorders also display a significant amount of passive-aggressive behavior. They often appear compliant and passive on the outside while feeling and often denying their deep anger and resentment inside. They then act out that hostility against their own bodies.

These are people who struggle constantly with issues of powerlessness and control. Often they experience themselves as totally helpless in a very frightening world. The overeating may symbolize their feelings of being out of control. It certainly reinforces the powerlessness.

Bulimics and anorexics often have major issues around perfectionism. They have bought into the notion that if they can control their exteriors, they can become more acceptable in their interiors, where they often feel fear, hurt, loneliness, and shame. The control they experience with food may be the only control they feel they have in their lives.

In Western culture, food is largely associated with nurturance. Children are routinely given food to soothe or as a reward. We are programmed from a young age to use food to fill our emptiness. Children literally hunger for love and approval, and when that is missing in their lives, food often becomes an alternative.

Eating disorders are referred to as "diseases of isolation.'' Those with eating disorders tend to have spent a tremendous amount of time in isolation filled with loneliness. As children they often experienced being alone as being abandoned. They internalized this feeling of abandonment as proof that they were not of value. Food became a substitute for human interaction. When parents weren't available, food provided the solace. But the fact that the hurt feelings weren't assuaged went unnoticed. Additionally, much of the behavior that fed their disorder was secretive, which created even greater feelings of loneliness and shame.

Eating disorders, particularly obesity and anorexia, can also be a way of calling attention to oneself—a way of expressing anger and rage; a way of rebelling and acting out. Compulsive overeating is often a way of pushing people away. Especially when one has been sexually abused, being overweight may be an attempt to keep people away to prevent further abuse. For anorexics, starving is a way of attracting attention while still keeping people at a distance.

It is important to recognize that in every eating disorder, the relationship with food becomes addictive. And, as with any addiction, the relationship to the addiction becomes the major focus in the person's life. Food addiction is much like any other substance and process addiction. It moves through:

- Loss of control
- Denial
- Increased dependence
- Change in tolerance
- Impaired thinking
- Preoccupation with and the control of the addictive substance

- Manipulation of one's environment to obtain the desired effects
- Lying
- Obsession
- Guilt and remorse
- Physical deterioration

Adult Child Issues

Research has clearly demonstrated that Children of Alcoholics are more prone to become chemically dependent. However, only recently have we begun to recognize that other compulsive and addictive behaviors can also be attributed to being raised in an alcoholic family. One of the most common addiction/disorders in American society centers around eating.

Reports indicate that 15 to 20 percent of the general population of women report eating disorders. It is widely believed that the majority of people with eating disorders are women. Yet it is my belief that men with food addictions are only just now being recognized. A disproportionate number of men and women with eating disorders come from physically or sexually abusing homes. In a study by Drozd, 1986, 59 percent of female ACOAs reported currently or previously having an eating disorder, as compared with 19 percent of the control group.[1] It will be of value for the reader to see how, in other chapters, compulsive overeating, bulimia, or anorexia were responses to physical and sexual abuse.

Adult Children often routinely medicate the pain of their past and of their present with food, becoming overeaters in the process. They fluctuate between the need to be in total control of their food intake and feeling totally out of control. Their poor self-esteem, often coupled with self-hate, contributes to self-destructive behavior that manifests itself in overeating, bingeing, purging, and starving. Once they are into these distinctive patterns of self-abuse, they shroud themselves in shame, and their need to hide and keep secrets becomes even more pronounced.

The Adult Child characteristics that appear to be integral to those with eating addictions are:

- Control and powerlessness
- Perfectionism
- Repressed feelings—particularly anger and shame
- Shame
- Needs

Control and Powerlessness. Children need to experience a sense of physical and psychological safety in their lives. They need primary caretakers to set healthy limits, to provide nurturance and support, and they need to have expectations that are appropriate for their age and experience. When parental figures do not establish the appropriate parameters and levels of control that produce a sense of safety, children accurately feel profound loss and powerlessness. They often act out that powerlessness, or they seek ways of controlling their lives by any means necessary. COAs struggle with their powerlessness on an ongoing basis. For many Adult Children, the intake or lack of intake of food is the only place in which their power lies. They seek control by attempting to manipulate what they have the power to affect. By finding the areas they can control, bulimics and anorexics learn to exert control and literally hang on for dear life. Overeaters also overfuel their bodies in an attempt to feel that they have some say over what they do.

Perfectionism. COAs often seek perfectionism in an attempt to be in control and/or mask shame. Sometimes areas they can affect are so limited, their only control rests with their bodies. Their preoccupation with needing to look good is often an external way of protecting themselves and protecting their families. If they look good, they believe their problems and those of their families will remain hidden from others. No one will be able to see beyond the false exterior to the real chaos and sickness in their lives. Starving and purging are clearly actions in pursuit of perfection.

Feelings. COAs are people who live with chronic fear, loneliness, hurt, and disappointment. They experience resentment and anger. They live with embarrassment and guilt—often believing that there's something terribly wrong with them. Theirs becomes a life of shame. Food offers solace, and it also deadens the pain.

Shame. Adult Children were raised with physical and emotional abandonment. They did not get the approval, the attention, or the love they needed. Very early they came to believe there was something extremely defective inside them, that they could never be good enough. If there had also been physical or sexual abuse, they experienced being treated as objects, not as people. These were major acts of boundary violation. Food anesthetizes the pain of the growing-up years and fills the emptiness that comes with past and present shame. Anorexics or bulimics often seek to escape from their feelings of inadequacy by driving themselves to perfect their bodies by starving and purging. Overeaters seek to compensate for their early abandonment by nurturing themselves with food.

Needs. These dysfunctional families are alcohol- and drug-centered rather than child-centered. These children learn that adults are not going to be available to attend to their needs on a consistent basis. They also find out that they can't even meet their own needs because they are just children. As a result, they learn to repress and minimize their needs, often becoming so good at it that they cease to be able to recognize their own needs. This behavior often brings on depression— a valid response to years of not having their needs met. But their depression makes them even more socially and emotionally isolated. Compulsive eating is a way of attending to those unrecognized needs as well as a response to the depression that is fueled as a result of needs not being met.

Life Stories: Growing-Up Years

Why is it some children develop eating disorders, others become chemically dependent, and still others develop different compulsive disorders? That's difficult to answer. However, once you look at an individual's history, the reasons usually become more obvious.

Some eating disorders reflect physiological predispositions. Just as there may be a chemical tendency toward alcohol and other drug addictions, there may also be a predisposition toward obesity. With eating disorders, you will often see that the adult was a child who tended to be more socially and emotionally isolated.

In the following stories, you will see that food played

a significant role from a very young age. Food was the mother's way of nurturing when she was bankrupt of other emotional resources. Dysfunctional parents often become preoccupied with food and body size and image in their need to control. For some, chronic childhood illnesses fed isolation, and food provided nurturance in times of stress.

The four Adult Children who are sharing their stories have had to struggle with eating disorders. Clearly, anorexia and bulimia are predominately female disorders. Males tend to fall into compulsive overeating that sometimes results in obesity. I've split the stories equally between men and women because as more men are entering Adult Child recovery, many of them are identifying compulsive overeating as a response to their Adult Child issues. These life stories illustrate how overeating, starving, and purging became responses to being raised in chemically dependent homes. Three of our life stories are about compulsive overeaters.

Skip was dangerously obese all through childhood—his top weight was 400 pounds. Yet for fifteen years now he has maintained an average weight of 170 pounds.

At the age of fourteen, Gloria came close to dying of anorexia. In her twenties she physically recovered to confront yet another level of recovery.

Felicia struggled with the meaning of food all during childhood, then became a compulsive overeater and finally bulimic. Gloria and Felicia reflect family histories of sexual abuse. Felicia and Skip are alcoholics.

Paul struggled with being "husky" as a child and twenty-five to fifty pounds overweight as an adult until he recovered in Overeaters Anonymous. The grandchild of an alcoholic, Paul was raised by two Adult

Children. His story is amazingly representative because so many people with eating disorders come from third-generation alcoholic families. His parents' Adult Child issues played a strong role in the development of Paul's eating disorder.

_____

SKIP
Age: 40
Mother: Co-dependent
Father: Alcoholic
Birth Order: Youngest of four
Raised: Indiana, Midwest
Socioeconomic Status: Middle class

_____

SKIP: "My father drank alcoholically until I was five years old. Then he stopped and went to Alcoholics Anonymous for one year. After that, he was a dry drunk with no emotional recovery. Although I have very little memory of my life from the time I was three until I was nine, I do have a sense that his 'not drinking' was so fragile that none of us in the family could breathe for fear he'd start drinking again.

"He'd come home from work, get on the couch, eat dinner alone at the coffee table, nap, and then go to bed. I remember feeling fearful, as if I needed to keep a lid on myself in order to avoid contact with him."

Skip describes his father as being abstinent, but with no emotional recovery. That occurs for various reasons, but the most common is that the alcoholic doesn't stay involved in an active recovery program. This is what happened to Skip's father. He went to AA for one year and then "stayed in control." He controlled himself by not drinking, and he controlled his family with his silence.

The fact that Skip cannot remember events from the time he was three until he was nine implies that his experiences of that time were overwhelmingly frightening. Sometimes the traumatic events that damage a child's sense of security and self-worth are overt—such as physical abuse. But the trauma is not so blatant in Skip's situation. Although silence is not often regarded as a source of significant trauma in a child's life, Skip and his siblings were subjected to their father's punishing silence. He was not just a quiet man—he was blatantly rejecting. His menacing silence was emotional torture to all the family members. A child developing a sense of identity and self-worth raised in an emotionally cold family internalizes the feeling that he must have caused this coldness. There must be something deeply wrong with him, something that makes people not want to respond to him.

Skip's description of "keeping a lid on" himself is an accurate metaphor for many children of troubled families. He needed to keep a lid on his feelings, on his emotional self. But, as a consequence, he couldn't keep a lid on the food. His need to control all his feeling manifested itself in his being controlling with food.

Skip's mother was a nurse. Since she worked the 11:00 P.M. to 7:00 A.M. shift, she had very little contact with Skip's father.

"I rarely saw them talk. Mother was nurturing and caring, but she also remained quiet and isolated. She worked very hard at her career, at home, and at church.

I always knew she cared for me, loved me. But I also knew that she was controlled by Dad.''

At dinnertime, Skip's dad was served his meal by his wife at the living room coffee table, in front of the television set. The four kids were served at the kitchen table.

''We sat down, ate, and left. Any talk was negative, derogatory, caustic. We hurled our hurt at each other.''

Skip's mom didn't sit at the table, she just kept moving about, doing things. In time, three of the four children ate themselves into obesity. Skip's sister and one of his brothers were also over two hundred pounds by their late adolescence.

Skip's mother was a co-dependent. Her own sense of powerlessness had to be severe for her to keep silent about her children's obesity—as both a mother and a health professional.

Although Skip remembers his mother as warm and kind, he still felt a sense of emotional abandonment as she continued her downhill spiral into helplessness. Yet although Skip knew that something was wrong with his family, he was unable to identify it.

''My dad didn't talk to me at all, and my mother wouldn't acknowledge that there was anything wrong. But my life was filled with this engulfing terribleness— and I thought it was me.''

Skip was screaming inside for someone to say something. This is the ''Don't talk'' rule taken literally.

"I wanted my father to tell me there was something wrong. I wanted him to tell me it was his fault. I wanted to hear it was not my fault. Later, as I got older I needed him to tell me he was proud of me. I didn't get any of those things.

"My home atmosphere was very frozen. I couldn't identify my feelings at that time, but I was constantly filled with the thought that whatever was wrong was my fault. I knew that we were all on our own in this family. My siblings and I were part of the family group, but each of us was alone."

Skip had trouble in school, beginning in the second grade when he developed a 20 percent hearing loss.

"School was a horror for me. It was only the occasional kind gesture from a teacher that would make me feel as if I could cope at all. When I developed my hearing problems, which were accompanied by severe headaches and infections, I discovered the pleasure of being home during the day, minus my father, and the peaceful solitude that brought. While my frequent absences also increased my sense of being out of place at school, what felt best to me was to be home during the day alone. It felt safe."

Even after his hearing problems were corrected, Skip continued to seek the safety of his solitude by feigning illness and staying home from school. This is when his eating began to take on emotional overtones.

"I would frequently order sweets from the milkman, and I continued in this pattern for years. Eating and

television were my friends, and there was a woman on a local talk show who became my mother/mentor.''

There was Skip, home alone watching television, finding comfort in his television friends, while the shows and commercials subtly, if not blatantly, reinforced the idea of food as a primary caretaker. Family shows such as *Leave It to Beaver, Ozzie and Harriet,* or, more recently, *The Brady Bunch,* demonstrating familial love, connectedness, and happy times with healthy eating—interspersed with ''M'm-M'm good!'' commercial invitations to eat—had to make Skip even hungrier.

Skip's solitude at home, coupled with his sense of differentness, kept him from making friends until high school. His relationships with his siblings were typical of an alcoholic family.

"My next oldest brother and I were close. I was less alone because of him. I do have a sense of his being on my side at times. My oldest brother was absent most of the time, mostly because he was very involved in sports. But I was also afraid of him because I didn't know him; he was a stranger to me.

"It was my sister, the oldest, who was my hero. She cleaned the house, made straight A's in school, and took care of me when I was young. She was the one who really raised me. Most of the nurturing I experienced came from her.''

Skip weighed 225 pounds by the time he was ten, which made him physically very different from the other children. His physical size alone would have put a distance between him and others. But he was also a COA—

and most of them, regardless of size, walk through childhood feeling different and separate from others.

Nevertheless, Skip began to look outside the family for support and companionship.

"There were many kids in my neighborhood, and they became important to me. I remember that I was always giving and doing for them, frequently buying them things and being a chameleon to their needs. This was where my main nurturing came from. Nurturing from taking care of others was a very early lesson for me."

It is a common story to hear of fat children giving their peers money—buying them things—in hopes of securing friendships. There is such a stigma in our society associated with being fat that few children want to be friends with a fat child.

Yet all children need and want friends. A sense of belonging is vital to a child's self-esteem. Skip was caught in the middle of a dilemma. He was struggling with being in a dysfunctional family where he felt no sense of belonging and also with having no sense of belonging among his peers because he was a fat child. The need to buy friendships makes sense when one feels unworthy and inadequate.

However, Skip did have two close childhood friends. Because he was so fat at such a young age, the buddies he acquired early on became long-term friends—he was unable to make new ones as he got older. But, as friends sometimes do, in adolescence Skip lost one of them to new and different interests. And this loss was directly connected to his weight.

"In high school, when my first friend became interested in girls, I felt left out. I was fat. I knew I couldn't compete in that world."

Already struggling with school—and life—Skip lost his one remaining friend to a fatal car accident when they were in high school.

"I was so unsupported and so unable to cope with my grief that I dropped out of school for a while. Ultimately it took me six years to finish high school. By this point I weighed four hundred pounds, which greatly added to my sense of inferiority."

The death of a dear friend at any age is a major loss. But to lose one's only close friend as a teenager is even more difficult. There is the sadness, the anger, the loneliness, the sense of abandonment. But there are also the existential questions of life and death: "Is dying painful?" "What is death?" "How did my friend feel about me?" The level of pain is overwhelming, and a child has no way of knowing if it will ever end.

Skip had nowhere to take his pain, nowhere to find solace—except in food.

The compulsiveness of his eating may or may not have been conscious. Skip may have been so disconnected from his emotional self that the pain may not have even registered emotionally. Yet it is at this time that he lost all control of his eating.

When Skip describes his family, it is with an eerie calm. It's as if he slowly and quietly gained his four hundred pounds without anyone's noticing. Yet four hundred pounds is a violent attack against one's body. It's difficult to imagine that one could launch such an offensive with no one in the family paying him any attention.

Skip was aware of feeling unremitting self-hate.

"I would constantly tell myself I was 'no good'; that I was a terrible person."

Most of Skip's conscious self-hatred had to do with the family environment. He was totally detached from his body image.

"When I was very young I told myself that as long as I stayed under two hundred pounds I'd be okay. By sixth grade I had passed that. But I let it pass without much recognition. I would stand in the mirror and only see myself from the head up. I didn't see my lower body at all. I would get obsessed with my hair. I had to make sure my hair was perfect, that it was combed and sprayed. If my hair was okay, then I was okay."

By the time Skip was sixteen, his father had begun drinking again—beer on weekends. He continued this until a year before his death.

Slowly, Skip moved emotionally into adulthood—under a cloud of sadness, with an inner core of hate and fear toward his father. Food quieted the anger and comforted the sadness.

"I was aware of nothing but an intense, overwhelming sadness. I would feel very sad in response to television shows, movies, and the stories that I would read. I can remember sometimes locking myself in the bathroom with some sad story and sobbing.

"In addition to the sadness, I had a lot of anger. It was

a conscious, internal hatred of my father that came through frequently. But basically, it was if I were in a functional coma all those years.''

_____

GLORIA
Age: 26
Mother: Co-dependent
Father: Pill-addicted
Birth order: Oldest of three
Raised: Northeastern city
Socioeconomic Status: Middle class

_____

Gloria was blatantly affected by several generations of alcoholism in her family. This meant that her parents had unacknowledged Adult Child issues of their own, which may have led to her father's chemical dependency.

GLORIA: "Many of my memories of my maternal grandfather are of his being sloppily, happily drunk at our many family parties. As a kid I may not have been bothered by this, but as I grew older I was annoyed by his messy speech and slobbering kisses. My mother and grandmother both denied for years that he had any problem. The women in my family are supreme nurturers/victims/deniers/martyrs. The men are fostered, protected, and made into gods.''

Gloria's paternal grandfather was also an alcoholic and very abusive. One of the still existing family secrets is that Gloria's father and his siblings were all chronically sexually abused by their father. Many times, as a young man, Gloria's father had had to knock out his father when he was on a drunken rampage. Out of the violence and pain of his own upbringing, Gloria's father developed a strong vision of what a family ought to be. In the end he became a controlling, tyrannical, pill-addicted autocrat.

"I didn't know that it was pills that were making my dad the way he was. I really never thought about why. I was just too scared. By the time I was born, my dad was already taking prescription medications. He kept the pills beside his bed in a drawer. Once, when I asked him about them, my mother clearly let me know I was not to tell my father that I knew about the pills. It was as if I was bad or wrong for seeing them. After she told me not to tell my father, she told me harshly: 'Get out of this room.' I understood it was a subject that was never again to be spoken about."

Gloria learned early in life that she should never do anything to disturb her father. Underneath his "master of control" demeanor, there was always the silent threat of violence.

"My mother taught me that, at all costs, I should never do anything to hurt my father or make him angry. I lived in constant fear of his awful silence that could, at the most unexpected moment, flare into red-faced rage. I have a mental image of myself in a crouch, like a dog that looks up pleadingly, hoping not to be beaten but expecting it, hoping to please the master but knowing it will never happen. The master will not, cannot, be pleased."

Every person in this chapter has had to respond to issues of control by their parents. For Skip and Gloria, parental control is perpetrated on the family in silence. The father's extreme silence had the power to instill immobilizing fear into all of the other family members. The "Don't talk" rule was enforced through silence.

As with many COAs, Gloria's feelings toward her father were very conflicted. He often spent time with her and gave her treats. But he was also unpredictable in his behavior toward her.

"My early years were spent both adoring and dreading my father. When I was very young, before I reached puberty, we would spend a good deal of time together, taking long walks, digging for fossils, watching Godzilla and Dracula movies. My father was the 'good guy,' the one who bought me Twinkies and soda, the one who spent money.

"But I would also get these terrible insults from my father. They were always delivered with a laugh. He'd tell me I was fat, ugly, and stupid. He would tease me incessantly. If I cried, he'd laugh. If I got angry, he'd laugh. Finally I decided never to show my hurt again."

When a parent is addicted to prescription pills, a child has greater confusion about their parents' usually hurtful and erratic moods and behaviors. Because children are less likely to relate the use of pills to their parents' behavior and the mood in the home, they are even more likely than most COAs to believe they are responsible for the hurtful feelings, that there must be something wrong with them. Shame begins early.

In these cases, the children often find the nonchemically dependent parent to be the "heavy." The chemically dependent parent may be easier to manipulate, may simply be absent, or at times may seem more fun or likable than the other parent.

"My mom was set up as the 'spoilsport,' the bad guy, the heavy. She was frugal—but I thought she was mean and stingy. She was careful about our eating well—but I thought her very disappointing as a mom. Other kids' mothers gave them sweets at lunch. I got an apple and maybe a plain oatmeal cookie."

It is possible that Gloria's mother's caution about food was her way of being the "good mother" or the "perfect mother." As her husband progressed in his illness, she had an even greater need to be "good" or "perfect." Her "goodness" was also a way of being in control. She demonstrated her "goodness" in other ways as well.

"To me, my mother appeared to be an extremely strong and overwhelmingly good person. I knew I could never be as unaffected, as noble, as unselfish, as she was. So I gave up my will to her. When we'd go clothes shopping, I'd let her choose my clothes. I would express no opinion at all, although I seldom liked the clothes she picked out."

Gloria eloquently describes what occurs for many COAs—they lose themselves in someone else. This is the beginning of her becoming invisible.

Gloria's best memories are with her brother Bobby, who is two years younger. Bobby was the funny, outgoing one. Although he had a violent temper, he usually kept it hidden. Most of the time he was affectionate and demonstrative. Gloria was quieter, less social, more reserved.

"Bobby and I played many imaginative games together with a whole troop of Christmas elves. We even took the trouble to divide the troop into two branches of the same family. It would take us hours to name the elves and then identify their family relationships. This was almost more important than starting the game. We shared a bedroom for many years, and we'd lie awake at night playing games and talking.

"One of my most poignant memories is of something that happened when we were both still in grade school. As we got ready for bed, Bobby wanted to kiss me good night. But I wouldn't let him; I refused to let him touch me. I had always hated being touched and to touch. But Bobby was always very affectionate, as was my mother. My mother was pleading with me to give Bobby a good-night kiss. Bobby was crying, saying that I didn't love him anymore.

"I lay on the bed, staring at the ceiling, 'knowing,' with the same awful certainty that I would later feel about eating food, that I could not kiss him—that if I had to kiss him, I would die. I would somehow cease to be. I didn't cry; I didn't feel anything about Bobby's pain."

Gloria had been able to let others know her physical boundaries nonverbally. But with Bobby she had to muster the strength to speak to her beloved brother. It is difficult to fully understand what touch meant to Gloria—but it clearly was frightening to her. She has no doubts about her love for this brother. For her to reject him in this manner meant this was her last stand of physically pushing people away.

Although Gloria has no memory of any sexual molestation, her father had been an incest victim—a fact that his wife wasn't aware of until twenty years after their marriage. Gloria described her father as very undemonstrative physically. He wouldn't let others touch him and wouldn't touch others.

"He refused kisses, he'd push you away, move his head; you couldn't touch him."

It is possible that Gloria needed to define her physical space in a manner that couldn't include others. She was responding to her lack of psychological safety—a chronic fear of some unknown rage. Her father provided the modeling—no touching.

In school Gloria was one of the "smart ones." She had a few special friends whom she would play with, other girls who were also good students.

"Grammar school was largely an unpleasant experience for me. My good memories of that time have to do with after-school activities. My family lived in an apartment, but my friends all lived in houses. I loved going to their homes because there was a good deal of privacy and often a yard to play in.

"By seventh and eighth grades, there was a lot of drinking going on at parties. I was never a part of the 'tough' crowd. My friends and I were the ones most often tortured and teased by them. I never dated or drank. I wore glasses and braces and was very shy around boys. I spent my eight years at that

school in fear—of both the students and the teachers."

Although Gloria continued to excel academically in high school, her sense of being an outsider became even stronger.

Solitude was something that offered comfort to Gloria. But in this solitude she also discovered the isolation that would soon lead to her eating disorder.

"I spent a great deal of time alone. On Friday nights, my favorite thing to do was sit at my desk, writing page after page of stories about girls my own age going on dates or learning about the facts of life. I also read lots of poetry and wrote verses myself, all of which rhymed. It wasn't until I was in high school and discovered the Beatles' lyrics that I started to experiment with 'free verse' and began writing more imaginative, less narrative poetry.

"In many ways, books saved me. Books gave me a world more real to me than the one in which I lived. I chose books for the fantasy and the challenges they offered me. I wasn't just a bookworm; I was a book vulture."

Part of Gloria's fantasy life centered around her image of herself as a caretaker.

"I would create a scene and then enter it. Usually there would be one or two girls, a few years younger than me, girls I knew by sight at school. I would be the 'mother/guardian' of those girls, and they would always be weak or helpless in some way, either physically frail or in some sort of trouble. I would order their world, keep it in check, and protect them."

Her fantasy was soon to become real—although she was the one who would be physically frail and in trouble. Her "trouble" was the end result of her trying to protect herself, of putting her world in order, of holding everything in check.

"In my freshman year of high school I must have heard the inevitable talk about diets. Girls that age are obsessed with how their bodies look. On some level something must have clicked: 'Ah, yes! Diet yourself to nothing! Martyr yourself. Starve yourself for attention!'

"I have no memory of making a decision to diet. But the following summer, when I was working at a day camp for the mentally retarded, I began to control my eating. Soon I was eating very little.

"From September of that year to January of the next I went from 105 pounds to 74. I was so physically weak I couldn't walk to school. I had lost nearly all of my hair. I was in such pain from the strain on my muscles that my mother had to spend hours rubbing my back. That was the onset of my anorexia."

Gloria's story is typical of many people with eating disorders. They are very disconnected—not only from their bodies, but also from their feelings and from any insights. Gloria had very little control over her life; her mother even picked out her clothes. She describes walking in her mother's saintly shadow as she is subjected to cruel teasing by her father. At home and at school, she always felt like an outsider. Self-starvation was a clear cry for help from a young girl who was dying on the inside.

PAUL
Age: 43
Mother: Adult Child
Father: Adult Child
Birth Order: Oldest of two
Raised: Midwest and California
Socioeconomic Status: Working class

Paul was born within a year of his parents' marriage. All the time he was growing up, he kept getting the message that, because of him, the family had been burdened with increased responsibility and financial problems. He always felt as though he had to make up for his early arrival.

At a very young age, Paul was expected to respond emotionally like an adult.

PAUL: *"I came into life immediately having to excuse my existence."*

In addition to obviously arriving earlier than planned, Paul was also a sick child. He had major health problems—rheumatic fever, pneumonia, chronic asthma.

"I was told that because of the medical costs, my dad had to work two jobs and limit his career goals and enjoyment of life. I remember my parents' joking about how I'd have to make a lot of money someday to pay them back for this sacrifice.

"From the beginning, I had the sense that I was the person responsible for all the family stress, and that I

was obligated to repay this somehow. As an adolescent, my major career goal was to make enough money to buy my parents a house, even though I knew that would not set things right. There was nothing I could do to repay them for the pressure and stress that I had brought into their lives.''

Both of Paul's parents were Adult Children, although neither became alcoholic. However, the family dynamics were no different from those of alcoholic parents. They simply continued to play out the dysfunctional scripts of their own childhoods. When you are an Adult Child, issues of control, inability to know what normal is, unhealthy boundaries and limit setting, need for approval, inability to make decisions, low self-worth, poor problem-solving skills, inability to listen, inability to play, and shame will gravely interfere with the ability to parent effectively. The inability to express feelings, issues of control, and unhealthy boundaries were all prevalent and hurtful to Paul.

"My dad's stepfather was an alcoholic. He was a harsh disciplinarian, uncaring, and mean. My father was always being blamed and always felt responsible as a child for everything that went wrong. He picked up that way of dealing with children and passed it on to my sister and me. I had this sense that I was obligated to him for the sacrifices he made for me. At the same time, I felt angry at not having had a choice. I relieved that guilt by overworking to try to deserve some good things.''

Paul's mother's father was also an alcoholic.

"My mother grew up bringing buckets of beer home for her father and raising all of her siblings. My mom had learned to worry and avoid conflict. She also had chronic health problems, and she would attack me as being heartless and cold-hearted when she felt I wasn't empathetic enough about her problems."

Paul was confused early about boundary issues. He wasn't taught to have an appropriate sense of who was responsible for what. His parents were unrealistic in their emotional and social expectations of him. They held him responsible for their feelings and their adult problems.

"Everyone was worrying about someone else's feelings and discounting their own. My mother would feel sad and worry about something going on with me. Rather than see that as my mother's sadness and worry, my father wanted me to be different so she wouldn't feel sad or worry. No one wanted to take responsibility for their own problems—they always blamed someone else."

As Skip had done, Paul would come to find that chronic illness played a significant role in his eating patterns. Because of his illnesses, he was often encouraged to eat to regain his strength.

"When I was seven, my sister and I stayed with my mom's parents for a few weeks. When my parents came to pick us up, they were shocked—we had both gained considerable weight. My grandmother had given us large dishes of ice cream at night to keep us from missing our parents and also to reward us for being well

behaved. At this point food had become not only necessary for my health, but also a reward and a soothing substitute for emotions.''

Paul attended Catholic school until the fourth grade, when his family moved from the Midwest to California.

"The school was run by nuns, who were great at instilling guilt and reinforcing the idea that children had to be responsible. We were even taught to feel guilty for feeling shame! We had to bring money for orphans and were told to pray at any free moment for the suffering souls. When we were caught talking in line, we were told souls were suffering in purgatory because we were not praying to get them out.

"I felt miserable about moving. And my parents only made things worse by letting me know that they were leaving home, family, friends, and jobs to go to California just because of me.''

Paul believed that his family moved to California because of his health. This only added to his guilt. It also inappropriately gave the issues of his health and food a lot of power.

A healthy family might also have made the same decision to move. But in a healthy family the parents would have taken responsibility for the decision. In Paul's family the adults were unable to do that. Instead they chose to hold their young child responsible for whatever went wrong from then on.

Guilt was burned into Paul's chest—a guilt that he understood all too clearly he'd never be able to get rid of. Like many COAs, he found that no matter what he did it wasn't going to be sufficient. He would never be able to be enough or do enough for his parents. In time food would become the only thing that symbolically allowed him to feel "full," "substantial," "worthy," "enough."

When the family moved to California, Paul began to attend public school.

"Again I was the outsider, trying to figure things out, trying not to make mistakes that would lead to embarrassment and family shame. I avoided competition, except in math. I was really quick with flash cards, so I'd compete in that area because I knew I could succeed. Sports competition was out of the question because I was not good enough.

"When I was in fifth grade, I had whooping cough and was out of school for several weeks. I remember coming home after my first day back and having a peanut-butter-and-jelly sandwich and a glass of chocolate milk to unwind from the stress of the day. That became a pattern, and I began to gain weight. When I got to the point where I needed 'husky boy' clothes, my mom began to express concern about my weight."

Eating after school is common for most children, but Paul was aware that he was eating in response to stress. The other issue was that his mother was going to try to control this part of his life.

Paul learned quite young that he could use his frail health to avoid doing physical activities that his parents wanted him to do. While his poor health made guilt a major theme in his life, he found that food could be an answer to his confusion and pain. At times he was able to vent his anger by using his poor health to his advantage.

"When my parents wanted me to fish, play Little League, or go to a social function, I would get sick to avoid it. I was scared of social situations. I was afraid of how I was supposed to act. I was angry that I was to go to please them. I was angry that they were always trying to control me."

Paul said he also played jazz and rock music very loud to deal with his anger. What he understood clearly was that it couldn't be expressed directly.

Paul and his sister got along fairly well. There was some competition, because Paul easily got A's, while his sister had to work hard for her B's. But she was the one family member with whom he tended to have a healthy relationship.

"I felt relief that there was someone in the family who didn't want me to parent or take care of them. I would feel good about my achievements with her and not worry about having to discount them to avoid hurting her."

As in many alcoholic families, mealtimes were stressful. Children with eating disorders often describe the need to eat all they can as fast as they can—and to get away from the table. Anorexics describe feeling so tense at mealtimes that they could eat very little. They would pick at food, push it about their plates, but eat nothing. Some children, often overeaters, describe not having any specific dinnertime and feeding themselves all evening long—potato chips, ice cream, macaroni and cheese, all starches and sugars.

"We generally ate our meals together, and they got pretty heated at times. To me, they were the great myth

*of what the family was supposed to be but was not. Mom
controlled conversations to avoid conflict between my
dad and me, while we chafed at the bit to do battle and
raced to see who could eat the fastest. This became a
habit for me—eating quickly without savoring or ab-
sorbing the food.''*

Paul was socially isolated for the most part while
growing up. Although he usually had one close friend,
that friend was often as lonely and isolated as he. Together the two would create their own fantasy world in
which to play.

*"My pattern was to find other outsiders and fuse with
them. In some way I would live vicariously through
them, especially if they had more of a social life. I
would gain access to social events through their friendship."*

*"In general, school was a place of stress. There were
the straight-A students, but I was always below them.
Socially I felt out of it with most groups. I felt I didn't
like what other people did for fun. Having gone to Catholic school, I was embarrassed by the open sexual behavior of the other students, and I didn't feel
comfortable at weekend drinking parties. What I
enjoyed doing, I did alone. I just felt strange and different.''*

Paul's illnesses kept him home a great deal, increasing his sense of isolation.

*"I never felt as if I fit in; I was always trying to adjust
to getting back to school. I got used to working at home
alone on schoolwork and then reading, or going off into*

fantasy, or watching television out of boredom. I was creating my own way out.''

Paul continued his pattern of isolating himself and eating. He would gain weight and then go on a diet. His parents would comment on his self-control, but then he would return to his old eating habits and the weight would come back.

Paul had been six feet tall from the time he was a freshman in high school. Being tall, he tended to look "big and husky," but not obese. But food had become his major focal point, and he perceived himself as "fat." However, pictures taken during his childhood show a youngster perhaps ten to fifteen pounds overweight, and in high school, he was about fifteen to twenty-five pounds overweight. But because of his parents' constant responses and comments, Paul perceived himself as fat and that something was wrong with him because of his size.

From the second grade on, Paul had a distorted body image, much like Felicia, whose story follows. He was overweight, and by high school he would be a compulsive overeater and would remain so. Although fifty pounds was the most weight he would gain, his whole life was preoccupied with food and body size.

Although Paul's parents may have been trying to be supportive by acknowledging his self-control, they quickly undermined this by being critical, emotionally distant, and blaming. Therefore he placed little value on receiving attention from them.

"Whenever the weight returned, it was back to dieting and feeling fat, disgusting, weak, unfit, undeserving,

*undesirable, and scared that I'd be fat forever, scared
that I would gain more weight.*

*"My childhood was mostly about fear and shame. I
was always so frightened of possible conflict. I also felt
I was responsible for my parents' terrible inability to
be happy."*

Paul lived in fear of taking on more and more guilt.
He was already carrying an enormous burden—the happiness of his entire family. This was exacerbated by the
shame he felt around the role of food in his life. The
burden became expressed in his body size.

FELICIA
Age: 41
Mother: Alcoholic
Father: Alcoholic
Additional Dynamic: Incest victim
Birth Order: Youngest of two
Raised: Texas
Socioeconomic Status: Upper middle class

Although both of Felicia's parents were alcoholic, she did
not recognize that drinking was a problem. Because her
family life had all the trappings of material success, she
assumed her parents' focus on drinking was "normal."

*FELICIA: "The days in our house focused on cocktail
hour, which began promptly at five P.M. On weekends
and holidays drinking began earlier, but 'never before
noon.' The air was filled with tension at all times, but*

I could never put my finger on what was wrong. I guessed it was something wrong with me.''

Looking back now, Felicia is able to see that the family was clearly alcohol-centered. Her parents were constantly preoccupied with the anticipation of drinking or actual drinking. The message was clear—the day began at cocktail hour. The kids were regarded as a "duty." They were attended to physically and materially, but emotionally they were abandoned.

The alcoholism in Felicia's family was covert, as it is in the families of many Adult Children. Felicia is the type of Adult Child who often says, "It wasn't that bad." In her case, both of her alcoholic parents were in the early stages of chemical dependency. The term *covert alcoholism* is often used to imply that the consequences are less tangible. But Felicia was responding to the alcoholism long before the signs of chemical dependency became blatant.

It is my belief that alcoholism always affects children negatively, whether the parents are in the early, middle, or late stages of chemical dependency. It is often denial that reinforces one's perceptions of covert or overt alcoholism. Felicia would clearly suffer from her mother's Adult Child issues and her chemical dependency; from her father's chemical dependency; and from her maternal grandfather's sexual molestation of her.

There is no such thing as "It wasn't that bad." The hurt and loss in this family are tremendous. Felicia's denial allowed her to minimize the effects of being raised in her family. It allowed her to avoid the pain.

Felicia's mother also came from a family with two alcoholic parents. In addition, her father was physically and sexually abusive. Because her mother's alcoholism was not blatant, Felicia was responding as much to her mother's criticism and negativity—all unresolved Adult Child issues—as she was to her mother's drinking.

Felicia's mother became even more critical and negative after 5:00 P.M., something Felicia now realizes was a result of her drinking.

"My mom was a very angry, controlling person. This certainly began in her childhood. And she did have reasons to be angry with my dad. He was very passive and didn't listen to her. He also acted as if he didn't need her, and all my mom wanted in her life was to feel needed. All I wanted was to at least be heard. I never was."

This generational cycle repeats itself not just physically, but emotionally. Both Felicia and her mother would become alcoholic, both focused on food and body image, and both were starved for love and attention.

Felicia's father wasn't very accessible while she was growing up. Through some shrewd financial investments he started his own real estate business, which was very prosperous. His work consumed most of his time. Cocktail hour began as soon as he got home from work.

Felicia feels that the only things with which her father was able to connect, with any sort of intimacy, were alcohol and food. Her father was overweight, and Felicia's mother was always trying to control his food intake.

"Overeating was a way to be like Dad. He was always sneaking food, and my mother criticized him constantly

*for this. Then I stepped into his shoes. I had finally
discovered a way to be like Dad and not like Mom; to
connect with Dad and to disconnect and distance myself
from Mom.''*

Felicia's eating patterns would come to be a struggle
in response to control by her mother and abandonment
by her father.

With hindsight, Felicia now sees that overeating,
mimicking her father's behavior, was a way of bonding
with him. Overeating was a wonderfully hostile response to her mother's controlling behavior. Eating,
when her mother was trying to control Felicia's intake,
was power.

Despite her father's unavailability, Felicia kept trying
to get closer to him, to connect with him, but she didn't
know how. She kept thinking that there was something
wrong with her.

*"I wanted to be like my dad. He seemed like a better
choice than my mom. At least he was rational and
funny. Mom was always so serious and so negative,
judgmental, and critical. She was always trying to
control Dad. I tried to protect him, but I failed. I tried
real hard at everything, but I was never enough.''*

The notion of limited supply pervaded Felicia's family life.

*"Was there enough vodka around for Dad's martinis?
Enough bourbon for Mom? Enough money? Enough time
for me? Enough love?''*

Unfortunately there wasn't enough attention and demonstrated love for Felicia to feel good about herself, so food became her fix.

Felicia says repeatedly that she was never good enough. She was never good enough to get her mother's approval or her father's attention. In time she would find food to be the only solace for the emptiness in her life. She would also discover that she could never eat enough to fill herself up. Her need could only be filled by the overt love and attention of her parents.

Felicia's mother was a housewife. Felicia grew up with a sense that she was always in her mother's way. She also felt a constant sense of disapproval from her mother.

"I just wanted her attention, and she was always too busy! She had to get food ready.

"My mother was also a perfectionist. She was pre-occupied with doing everything right. Nothing was ever good enough for her. I remember my mother coming into my room and pulling clothes out of my drawers and then telling me to clean up my room. I felt as if nothing were mine, that at any point I would be sub-jected to close scrutiny and made to feel inadequate."

Felicia was living in a family where she was emo-tionally abandoned. By age six this vulnerable, needy child was being periodically molested by her grandfa-ther.

Felicia and her sister were sent to live with her mother's family—although her parents knew they were alcohol-ics—for some weeks when her father became seriously ill and needed to be hospitalized. During this visit her grandfather sexually molested her. For the next six years

Felicia's grandfather would come to town one or two times a year. He would "help the family out" by taking Felicia places. He continued to molest her on these outings. Felicia remembers little of what happened when they were together, but she does remember the fear, shame, and humiliation she felt.

Eating disorders are not just a frequent response in Adult Children of Alcoholics, they are also common among survivors of sexual abuse. Food—compulsive overeating, bingeing, and starving—meets the same emotional needs when one is the child of both an alcoholic and sexually abusing family, and the likelihood of an eating disorder occurring in such a case is even more pronounced.

Felicia already understood that there was something wrong with her. She knew she seemed to be a constant problem to her parents—that, basically, they didn't want to hear from her. She couldn't go to her parents and tell them about the molestation; her parents had sent her to her grandfather's in the first place. Her grandfather was someone she was supposed to love. Felicia's response to the incest was to be compliant and to quickly pretend it didn't happen. She shut down emotionally: Don't think. Don't feel. Just eat.

It was shortly after this that Felicia began to love sugar.

Felicia's parents were very good about providing for her materially, and at the age of seven she turned to horseback riding as a way of winning attention and praise. She would compete in riding events, often for candy bar prizes. It was at this time that she began to get fat.

"I usually won the races I competed in, and I brought my trophies home—on my body. I got the praise I was

*hungry for, but I felt as if the hugs were for what I did,
not who I was.''*

In addition to being an excellent horseback rider, Felicia was a very good student.

*"Overall, school was always a positive experience for
me. I did well, and my parents approved. We all had
high expectations for me. I was a year younger than the
other kids in my class, so socially I was immature. But
my grades were good and seemed to be all that was
important.''*

Felicia was learning that looking good and performing well was what her parents valued. The more she became conscious of that, the more she felt ignored and nonvalued. She was starving for love, but she felt as if she were simply a decoration for her parents. In her conflict to get love and approval, she would continue to perform, but she also sabotaged the "looking good" with overeating.

Felicia spent much of her time alone, riding. When she wasn't practicing for a competition, she would ride her horse out into the woods, then find a place to sit and read. She was most comfortable by herself. This was not a sign of self-acceptance, but one of isolation based in fear, a lack of acceptance, and shame.

In Felicia's family the alcoholism was more subtle because the trauma was not yet blatant. Nonetheless, she was experiencing abandonment on a chronic basis. Her emotional needs were being consistently ignored as a result of her parents' alcoholic personalities. Also, she was repeatedly molested by her "trusted" visiting grandfather during these years.

Although isolation had become a way of life for her, by the time she entered high school Felicia began to feel the pressure to be like the other kids. It was during her senior year in high school that drinking became a part of her social life. She and one of her friends would go out on a regular basis and "party."

"Alcohol and food was the glue that bound our friendship. She was my drinking buddy, and I was hers. By the time I began college, most of my friendships revolved around using alcohol and pot. I was too scared and too much in control to use LSD or other heavy drugs. Alcohol was 'okay.' But I was not okay when using it. I began to be scared that I might have a problem."

The Role of Food

Food often plays a very significant role in the lives of children from alcoholic families. It can offer solace to the child who is feeling hungry for love or attention. It can be a friend for the child who feels isolated and alone. A child who develops an eating disorder often substitutes food for the intimacy that is lacking in the family.

However, when these children become overweight, they can find the issues of growing up in an alcoholic family doubly difficult. Self-esteem erodes even further, and self-loathing increases. The child feels the shame twice over—both for the alcoholism in the family and for his or her "ugly" body.

Overeating is another way of "stuffing" your feelings, something Children of Alcoholics learn to do at an early age. The child may wish to be "invisible," but the overeating is also a cry for attention. As one Adult Child puts it, "It's a way of killing yourself with food."

Anorexics may be trying to become less and less visible in order to hide from the inner pain. They may be reacting to the lack of control in their lives, and food intake becomes the one area in which they have some power.

There is also the problem of never feeling as if you're good enough. Becoming anorexic is often a striving after perfection—the perfect weight, the ideal body image. Unfortunately, perception of one's body usually becomes distorted.

The withholding of food may also be a form of punishing oneself for being "bad." In fact, both overeating and starving can be forms of self-punishment. Bulimics struggle between the two. They flip-flop between being out of control in their use of food to comfort and punish and being overly controlling in seeking perfection—the way they present themselves to the world.

In recovery, you have to be able to identify the role that food—or lack of food—has played in your life.

Role of Food for Skip. In both childhood and adulthood, food was Skip's best friend. Food was solace. It was nurturance. It helped to anesthetize the pain. But it was also a source of added shame.

SKIP: "People stared at me; I couldn't fit into chairs. The way I felt about my body, the way I felt about me, just increased my sense that something was wrong with

*me. I had absorbed all the uncomfortableness of my
family in those four hundred pounds.''*

Felicia says that *feeling* fat was a symbol of her
shame. For Skip, *being* fat was the symbol of his shame.
Here is a 225-pound ten-year-old boy; 400 pounds by
his late teenage years. Skip is screaming for help! But
his family is so frozen in silence, the only way he or
his siblings can speak is through their overeating—and
still they are ignored!

*"Prior to my recovery, eating was always secretive. I
would eat mainly at night, nonglorious food like peanut
butter and bread, bacon and eggs. My secretiveness
with food also extended to stealing food from friends'
refrigerators, eating off other people's plates as I carried them from the table, eating things I rescued from
kitchen trash bags.*

*"Privately I ate to fill myself and quiet my pain. Pub-
licly I ate in a manner that would allow me to avoid
attention from other people. I would eat moderate help-
ings, a salad, no dessert. I would be as invisible as
possible. I felt so unworthy in my life that I had to
counter any rightful healthy attention I could receive.
Then, privately, I would counter that positive attention
with negative feelings about what I was shoveling in my
mouth.*

*"Even when I was an adult and rapidly losing my
weight, my sneakiness continued. I would be at a dinner
party and I'd find a reason to leave the table and sneak
into the kitchen. I'd find a spoon, get to the freezer, find
the ice cream, open it up, gulp down large tablespoons,
put the lid back on, clean up the spoon, and wipe my
hands because ice cream can often be messy. Then I'd*

calmly return to the dining area without the other guests being aware of my behavior.

"Throughout all this, I was constantly trying to lose weight. Every month I'd start a new diet; it would last from three days to two weeks. I was obsessed with this constant yo-yoing. It was a very effective tool for avoiding myself, which is what I had been trained to do."

Many people with eating disorders become as addicted to dieting as they are to eating. But the dieting is just another attempt at control—one that is usually doomed because the emotional component of the addiction is not being addressed.

Role of Food for Gloria. Gloria's eating disorder occurred so quickly that she has little memory of that time. Her inability to remember is part of being so removed from her feelings, as well as the disorientation and confusion that is created by starvation. In retrospect, with therapy she is aware of feeling that if she ate food, she would cease to be; food would suffocate her.

GLORIA: "I never thought about food until the crisis was on me. I do know my mom was very careful about our eating. At school I was teased a lot about the strange foods in my lunch box. The other kids always had peanut-butter-and-jelly sandwiches on white bread. I had health foods and whole-wheat bread. I would get angry with my mother for being so different and making me feel so different.

"Also, my dad and grandfather often told me I would get fat and never get a husband if I kept eating so much.

*I always liked food, but I didn't carry extra weight. All
I knew was, I was doing something wrong."*

Gloria was fighting for her life, but, ironically, in
doing so she was also killing herself. She wouldn't eat
because she was afraid that if she did, she wouldn't
know herself. She had very little sense of her wants or
her feelings—it wasn't safe to know them. Yet she literally hungered to find herself.

*"It wasn't until I began to 'diet' that I began to obsess
about being thin. It began by my eating very little, and
by eating in a very ritualistic way. I would forbid myself
all the foods I loved and would exercise compulsively."*

At the onset of her anorexia, Gloria, who was five
foot six inches, weighed 105 pounds. Within six months
she was down to seventy-four pounds. She lost her body
hair. She lost the fat pads on the bottoms of her feet.
She was too weak to walk. She suffered from muscle
pain. And she was so severely dehydrated that her skin
became chapped and broken, resulting in scars. Gloria
was in desperate need of help.

Role of Food for Paul. Paul chronically felt left out,
alone. As with Skip and Felicia, he never felt he was
good enough. In addition, he felt totally responsible for
his family's unhappiness. Finding no way to feel good
about himself, he made food his best friend.

Compulsive overeaters develop a love-hate relationship with food, and a self-hate relationship lies in the
nurturance and solace that food provides. It helps to
take the eater's pain away. The hate relationship develops because the food becomes a source of shame. It

represents a loss of control and powerlessness that feeds an already deep-seated shame.

PAUL: *"Can a bowl of ice cream be your major sensual experience of the day? For me, ice cream became a tool for self-nurturing. Food was a comforting friend, a sexual friend, that deadened the feelings of stress, anxiety, worry, perfectionism, anger, shame, guilt, and embarrassment. I could relieve those tensions with soothing foods."*

While Skip disassociated from his body, Paul was very focused on his body.

"As a child I was sick and weak and warned that I'd have a 'chicken chest' if I didn't learn to breathe better through my asthma attacks. When we got to California I remember feeling embarrassed about taking my shirt off or wearing shorts because of my pale skin and flabby upper body. Swimming lessons were painfully embarrassing and frightening.

"As I gained weight, much of it was in the thighs and buttocks, so buying pants became very traumatic. I always had to buy large-waisted ones with wide legs. And then I had to try them on to see if they were cut full enough. So now I was self-conscious about the lower part of my body, too. To top it off, I developed breasts because of the fat."

Every fat child has stories of shame about clothing. If shopping can be avoided, it will be. Clothing styles are a part of fitting in, an essential element in belonging. Fat children can't wear stylish clothes. Skip's mother bought his clothes at an outlet that sold uniforms.

For adolescent boys, competing in sports is almost a rite of passage. Any boy who dislikes athletics and is not very developed athletically struggles to some degree with his self-esteem and image. Being overweight creates even greater difficulty in this struggle.

"I felt physically incompetent in sports because of my weight. Early on I withdrew from competition, so I did not develop any skills. That gave me an ongoing self-definition of 'fat kid' in PE. It was also how the coaches and other kids saw me. Showering in the gym was horribly embarrassing."

Teens differ in the timing of their sexual development, but they all agonize to some degree over what is right for them. Feeling anxious, confused, and fearful is a natural part of the process. But the COA has an even greater struggle because of mixed messages regarding sexuality. Adding a distorted, negative body image to one's emerging sexual feelings creates even more confusion and fear.

PAUL: "Sexually, I felt unattractive. Food helped me over the lonely weekends, while simultaneously making me feel even more undesirable. I was an awkward loner who already felt self-conscious with girls. The weight just added to my negative self-image. My sexual fantasies focused on forcing girls to have sex. The idea of some girl wanting to be sexual with me never entered my mind.

"I'd practice playing basketball, volleyball, badminton, and tennis—but I practiced them alone, except for school

PE classes. The one good thing was that I was tall. When I felt good, I would see myself as tall, thin, strong, and limber. But when I felt bad about myself, I'd see my body as fat, dumpy, and weak. The confusing part was that my head said I was fat whether I was or not.

"Growing up in my family gave me a painful and scary view of the world. Food became my only means of escape from the feelings that view produced."

Paul's food and COA issues are similar to Skip's and Gloria's. But Skip's compulsive eating resulted in obesity and Gloria's in anorexia. Paul was a compulsive overeater who internalized an image of being fat and not good enough that would become part of his yo-yo cycle of dieting.

Role of Food for Felicia. Despite her mother's careful restriction of her diet, Felicia got very mixed messages about food. Still, her problems with food did get her attention—and that was the important thing.

FELICIA: "Food was love. Food was attention. Food was a way to connect with my dad and break away from and rebel against my mom. Food was the answer. Food was the solution. Food was also a friend.

"My mother controlled my food. My sister could eat cookies, peanut butter, and ice cream while I could not. She could have hamburgers and hot dogs. I got only the meat. At the time I couldn't feel anything, but I now know that I felt deprived, as though there was never enough of anything."

Felicia got the attention she wanted. But it was negative attention that sliced away at her self-esteem.

"The same mom who controlled my diet also fed me whenever I was sick, happy, proud, sad, angry, or even just uncomfortable. She'd always say, 'You must be hungry. You need to eat. With a full stomach, you'll feel better.' Eating, not eating, gaining weight, losing weight—anything and everything about food got me attention. With food I was the center of the universe. I got the attention I craved."

To be fed as a response to all one's needs, whether physical or emotional, makes it difficult for anyone to differentiate hunger from other bodily signals. Felicia was primed to see food as the answer to all of her unspoken needs.

The issue of control is major for all ACOAs. For Felicia, control and food were all bound up together.

"My childhood relationship with food was all about control. My mom controlled everything I put in my mouth, or at least she tried to. I didn't learn to control or manage my own food. All I learned was how to rebel, how to sneak, how to be dishonest with her and ultimately with myself. And I felt such shame, even then."

Felicia's shame reflects not only her perception of her body as "not right," but also her dishonesty and low sense of self-esteem. Not only does this create problems for Felicia around food, it also teaches her not to trust her own perceptions. She learns that she cannot trust others to meet her needs. To get what she wants, she has to manipulate and deceive.

Compared with Skip and Paul, Felicia was closest to

an average body size. Although she felt fat, she was only somewhat overweight, not obese.

"In high school, I felt fat. I realize now that feeling fat was synonymous with feeling insecure and lousy about myself. Feeling fat had little to do with what I looked like or how much I weighed. Feeling fat was the symbol of my shame."

Food was also a solace for her shame and humiliation about the incest. Food was her friend at a time of much fear, shame, and loneliness.

Food played an early role in the dysfunction of these COAs. Although some people with a childhood eating disorder attend to it during their youth, for most, treatment and/or recovery doesn't occur until adulthood—if at all. When food addiction begins in adulthood rather than childhood, it usually fills the gap left by the cessation of another primary addiction, such as chemical dependency or workaholism.

Felicia found she needed to get sober first before she could deal with her issues around food. Skip recognized his chemical dependency only after recovery from his food addiction. Gloria recognized her food addiction at age fourteen—only to be confronted with the symptoms of yet another food addiction in her twenties. One addiction often masks another, and one addiction often replaces another. In these life stories, three of four people were adults before they could recognize and actively address their food addiction.

Life Stories: Adulthood and Recovery

SKIP
Age: 40
Compulsive overeater
Occupation: Psychotherapist
Recovery Process: Self-help, therapy

Skip continued to live at home after he graduated from high school.

SKIP: "For the first few years after high school, I made no attempt to work. My parents silently accepted my being there. My brothers also stayed at home, but they both worked. Finally, when I was twenty-three or twenty-four, I ventured out and got a volunteer job as a teacher's aide. I didn't believe I was worthy of any pay."

Food continued to be an answer for Skip. Very little changed in his life during these years, aside from increasing loneliness, sadness, and shame. Then, when Skip was twenty-five, his father had heart surgery and died of complications resulting from the operation.

"When my father died, I initially feigned remorse, but that lasted only a few moments. Then I felt an incredible sense of freedom, a glimmer that I was normal, I wasn't awful, that I had self-worth. I began to realize I had strength. Suddenly I felt important in my family. I planned the funeral. I settled the estate. I took care of

*the bank accounts. At my father's funeral, my uncle
mentioned to my mother that she might need to make
some provisions for me regarding my care. But now I
was helping to take care of the family."*

Skip's isolation and weight were so apparent that his
uncle assumed he would need to be provided for finan-
cially. To the outsider Skip's inability to function was
apparent. Yet until his father died, nothing was ever
said. Skip's father had been given tremendous power by
his family members. But the moment his father died,
Skip immediately reclaimed his power.

Unless there is some type of outside intervention, it
usually takes an event as powerful as the removal of the
source to create change. Yet even then many people
have such a deep-seated sense of helplessness that they
may be immobilized and unable to respond as Skip did.

It was as if Skip could find no identity, no value in
himself, as long as he felt his father's presence. His
response was to numb all of his feelings, to kill himself
slowly with food. The larger he became, the greater
became his need to remain isolated; he had to respond
not only to his family's dysfunction, but to the deep,
internalized shame he experienced because of society's
view of fat people.

*"After my father died, it was as if his toxicity died,
too. Somehow my inner child was reconnected with
my Higher Power. I had the sense that I was no longer terrible. My father's constant silence had given
me a clear-cut message—he hated me. I compounded
that by eating and putting on weight in order to feel
hateful.*

"After his death, however, I began to realize that

I didn't need food the way I had in the past. After seven months I had lost over one hundred pounds. Without my father's constant presence, I was able get a true sense of myself. For the first time I knew that my body wasn't representing to the world who I really was."

Skip got a job working at a children's home. Two of his co-workers, both male, offered him positive role models of unconditional acceptance. He continued to lose weight. After working there for four years, Skip left and took a part-time job working for a nationally based diet center. It was through this job that he saw the benefits of counseling.

"I got a lot of affirmation from my class there, but eventually I had to leave because I wasn't comfortable with their system any longer. I continued to work in the child-welfare field and began two years of Gestalt training. Through this, I went into therapy with one of the counselors from the training. I also heard about the Adult Child self-help program and began to attend meetings."

By this time Skip's weight had been drastically reduced. On the other hand, his drinking had increased. This is not a surprising progression. First of all, Skip is biologically at high risk because the sons of alcoholic fathers are more likely to become alcoholic than any other identifiable group of people. Second, without a recovery program for an eating disorder, people often replace one addiction with another. Skip was involved in a healing process, but it wasn't an active recovery program for his food addiction. By placing himself in a nontoxic environment, he was growing. He had healthy, caring people in his life. But he had not yet dealt actively with his shame. All the repressed feelings of his childhood were still there to haunt him.

"I was feeling better and beginning to succeed. But I was also beginning to drink. I was continuing a lifelong pattern of abusing myself and also sabotaging my career success. I even flirted with suicide on occasion by drinking and driving. Another time, I took both alcohol and pills, hoping to die but wanting it to be seen as an accident. I was going through a real inner struggle. Finally I crashed. It was then that I entered a treatment program for co-dependency and alcoholism."

A therapist at the treatment center identified the alcoholism, although Skip was initially very resistant to the label.

"I felt it meant that I wasn't in control, that there was one more thing I had to give up, that I was wrong, and, even worse, that I was like my dad. Yet the facts were there—I was clearly self-destructive in my drinking.

"The woman therapist who confronted me about my drinking also played a significant role in helping me struggle through my resistance. I knew something major was happening at this point because, for the first time in my life, I believed that people truly loved me for just being me. I was feeling unconditional love. In the beginning, I'm sure I continued my sobriety for her. This was not romantic love I was experiencing. It was the realization that another human being truly found value in me, and I didn't want to do anything to mess that up."

Six months after that Skip was sober, and after doing a great deal of work on his own, he began to attend AA meetings. Later on he also began attending Overeaters Anonymous meetings. In both cases he continued to feel out of place and very self-conscious.

"I didn't feel as if I was good enough to warrant the help of others."

Dealing with his food addiction proved much more difficult than dealing with his addiction to alcohol. Yet it was in OA that Skip felt an identification more quickly. After some time in this process, he started to attend ACOA meetings. All three groups continue to be a part of his recovery program.

Although self-help meetings have been integral in his recovery, Skip first accepted and surrendered to his dependency in an inpatient co-dependency program. Since then he has participated in psychotherapy and also in reconstruction therapy. The reconstruction workshops he refers to are usually a therapy environment in which a group of people work specifically on co-dependency issues. This is generally an intense therapy experience of working together daily over several days (often three to eight). Role playing and psychodramatic therapy techniques coupled with group process create an intensely cathartic experience that facilitates inner healing. It was there that Skip finally focused on his anger.

"Anger was the feeling that frightened me the most. My own anger was by far the most difficult and most important feeling I had to 'own' for my recovery. Owning my anger was the only way I could reclaim my childhood.

"Expressing anger was difficult for me because I'd learned very early that it wasn't safe to talk about anything. The rules in our house were: 'Don't talk. Don't lose control.' I had only heard my parents fight once, and then it was a very moderate argument. I didn't believe that I had the right to be angry. I wasn't worthy. I thought I had to settle for the little I had. In order to work through my anger, I had to reclaim my child from my dad.

"Today, recovery means taking care of my inner child. It means recognizing my many feelings and my needs and nourishing them with attention and respect—not with food. It means reintroducing little Skip to my mother, who has begun her own recovery process. Finally, I'm beginning to get the maternal nurturing I needed and deserved as a small child.

"Other Adult Child issues I've had to work on are control and powerlessness. Eating became the only way I could keep busy and avoid myself, since I thought I was so terrible. Nowadays, without my food dependency, I am not able to feel as bad. Without food, I am not overly controlling. I am learning to face the good things about myself rather than feeling self-hate. Without my food, I lose my main incentive to think strictly in terms of black and white. My life now has meaning beyond merely dieting and bingeing.

"I've managed to stay connected with my mother and my sister. My sister and I are still close, and she too has begun a recovery process.

"Today, I operate a great deal from feelings. I do what I want to do. I now understand that I am important, and that my own needs have to come first. My life is balanced between work, play, solitude, and friendships—my family of choice. In any twenty-four-hour pe-

riod, I usually have some contact with all those areas. If I miss any of those parts of my life, it tends to be play, but generally I have a balanced life.

"My body image is where my last real pieces of work have been focused. I feel great sadness for the stress I have put on my body. I also have a great regard for my body for 'staying with me' and helping me survive. My body and little Skip are very connected, and I find it very important to keep expressing my love and appreciation of them. I've even allowed myself to have some cosmetic surgery in the last few years. It's taken such a long time to give myself the attention I deserve. Every day now I'm grateful and happy for myself and my body in some way or another."

GLORIA
Age: 26
Compulsive eater, anorexic
Occupation: Copywriter
Recovery Process: Therapy

When Gloria was fourteen her anorexia was so completely out of control that many people openly confronted her parents, particularly her mother, about how sick Gloria looked. One day Gloria saw a television report about anorexia and identified herself. She went to her mother, telling her what was wrong and asking for help. She asked her parents to put her in a treatment program.

GLORIA: "I remember becoming rapidly and horribly unhappy with my diseased life. I didn't understand what was happening to me or why. I wanted very badly to be well, and I was very upset with the whole thing. I also knew I couldn't do it on my own—I was way out of control. I knew that the only way I could get better was with the help of my family.

"I asked to be taken out of my home and put in a program run from a hospital. It took my family many visits to different doctors to find the therapist who really saved my life. Although this occurred before there was much public awareness of eating disorders, my parents did find a therapist who was an expert in the field."

In spite of their dysfunction, Gloria's parents ultimately had the ability to respond to the fact that their daughter was dying. Gloria said her mother had been angry with her for months for not eating, but that she'd seen Gloria as being willful. Yet pride, fear, and ignorance did not get in the way once they thought they had a diagnosis for what was wrong—anorexia.

Gloria continued to see her therapist regularly on an outpatient basis for the next two years, and she quickly responded to treatment.

"I immediately liked this therapist. I saw him two times weekly and then once a week for over two years. I was so sick that I missed school from December through March, but I felt hope. I was silent for a long time in my sessions. I didn't know what to say. I didn't know there was anything inside of me. But he talked to me, and I began to eat for him. He told me I had to."

Gloria's therapist was a wonderfully safe person for her. She remembers a trust exercise he once did in which he picked her up and set her down.

"I was willing to let him touch me. I let him pick me up. But all the while I knew he was going to drop me. I waited for him to drop me. And he didn't. I was astonished—he didn't drop me!"

Gloria was learning about safety, about trust. In many ways her therapist became a surrogate father. Within six months her physical state was stable. However, she has never regained all of her muscle strength, nor the fat pads on the soles of her feet. She can still see scars when her skin is cold and chapped. Her hair has never been as full as it was.

After completing high school, Gloria went on to college. At twenty-six she has spent nearly all of her adult life in college. For the past two years she has been a copywriter in an advertising agency.

Gloria was very young when she began her recovery. At the age of fourteen, however, she lacked the years and the emotional and mental resources to experience the emotional recovery she would later desire. Although the therapy during high school literally saved her life, she would need to address many more issues in her young adulthood.

"When I began college I was still thin, fearful of being fat, and had difficulty gaining weight. But in my junior year I was under so much stress that I began to overeat.

"Food was never an innocent pleasure for me. There was always the fear of overeating. And now that's just what I was doing. I clearly ate to punish myself. I wanted to punish myself for all the negative things I was feeling about myself—anger, hurt, pain. I would eat alone when no one else was home. I'd take the phone

*off the hook. There was this ritualistic feel to it all. Now
I was lord and could eat as if I were Henry the Eighth
or an Amazon queen.''*

This compulsive binge eating was a signal to Gloria
that her eating disorder wasn't over. As with any addiction, recovery was an ongoing process. Gloria would
need to deal with her recovery issues on a continuing
basis.

*"I realized that I had to abandon the dreadful cycle of
guilt and punishment: that I had to reject self-abuse.
For me, part of this healing has meant strengthening my
friendships with older women, working out my issues
with the other women in my family, learning to love
myself as a woman, and realizing my own strength. As
both a Catholic and a recovering Adult Child, I still
had vestiges of the saint syndrome: 'One must be all
things to all people.' This was certainly reinforced by
the role women played in my family.''*

Gloria needed to learn to love herself as a woman
and to realize her own strengths. Eating disorders are
often a feminist issue because many women in our
society base their self-image on men's perceptions and
value of them. At this time in our history, ''Thin is
in.''

Culturally, women are defined and learn to define
themselves by their body size and physical attractive-
ness. For many women, feeling fat is often equated with
the belief that one is horrible and worthless. Although
men can and do suffer from food addictions, they are
not so quick to build their self-esteem solely on body

size. They also create value around athletics, job status, and material possessions.

One of the main issues Gloria has had to deal with is her old need to feel "smaller" than a man, if only physically.

"While this is just an old habit for me, it is still hard to break. I feel at peace with myself, with my own intellectual and emotional powers now. But it's hard to get rid of the idea that the thinner one is, the lighter one feels, the faster one moves, and the more graceful one appears. When I'm involved with a man, I still eat less than I normally would, even though the man will usually say that I could stand to gain some weight.

"It annoys me that eating is still a 'problem' for me. However, I am much less hard on myself now than I've ever been. If I eat too much, instead of loathing myself and calling myself a stupid pig, I talk to myself in a soothing manner. I forgive myself and try to figure out why it happened."

Gloria's old sense that if she doesn't stay extremely thin she'll cease to be is becoming much weaker. It's an old habit, an outworn point of view, based on over-emphasizing the superficial aspects of her self-image.

"Taking care of myself is a relatively new idea for me, and one that I am working on to make a healthy new habit. When I was young I used to test my endurance in lots of small ways. For example, I'd leave the car window wide open on a cold night and let the icy wind whip my face numb before I'd close it. Now I take along gloves in sixty-degree weather, just in case I get cold. Another way I take care of myself is to eat three meals a day instead of one.

"I'm working on a number of issues now:

- *Self-care—truly taking care of myself.*
- *Respect—having real regard for my own intelligent, heartfelt choices.*
- *Self-reliance—learning to believe in and rely upon myself.*
- *Trust—learning to trust my feelings and judgments and to trust other people.*

"Two years ago, at work, someone showed me the twelve questions that help someone know if he or she is an Adult Child. I immediately answered 'Yes' to all of them. I've always been looking for balance. 'All or nothing' behavior has been my norm. I've always had trouble with personal boundaries. And I've always been a sponge for the energies of others.

"So much of my life I had no sense of my own space. I was hardly in my own body. I had trouble keeping my own secrets. I would tell people my secrets to purchase intimacy. I've never been malicious—only pitiful. Being an amoeba describes me as well. I easily merge into others. Recently I've been learning to feel and be separate from others. Now I can set healthy boundaries.

"I'm also on much better terms with my issues of control and powerlessness. My entire life I've struggled with my feelings of powerlessness. Rigid control was my only answer. Today I speak my feelings—no more self-distrust. Today I have a sense of me. As I connect with others more and more, I'm finding my own strength. And I'm also finding strength through my love of nature and the arts."

Gloria had been starving for validation and attention, as is the case with so many other COAs. And, as with the others in this chapter, food was an attempt to meet those needs. For Gloria, depriving herself of food was a cry for help that symbolized her emotional starvation.

"I am seeking to find the strength to stand alone, but not be isolated; to know who I am separate from others. I'm learning self-respect and how to provide my own sustenance. In my next love relationship with a man, I hope not to be so pliable, so good, so forgiving, so ready to care at all costs. For years I could not be intimate. But lately I've been too ready—still moving from one extreme to the next, from a stone to a blade of grass.

"I'm continuing to work on acknowledging and showing my strengths, on admitting my full worth."

PAUL
Age: 43
Compulsive overeater
Occupation: College administrator
Recovery Process: OA, Al-Anon

Paul began attending junior college after he graduated from high school. During this period he became more and more aware and resentful that his father was trying to find his own identity and worth through possible accomplishments of Paul's. Paul deliberately chose a college path that was not as apt to lead to a high-paying career by majoring in sociology. Later, when he received his bachelor's degree and then his master's, he deliberately did not attend graduation ceremonies in order to deny his father the opportunity to gloat or take any credit for this achievement. Although Paul's anger may not have been readily apparent to him, it was close to the surface.

Up to this time Paul had been a social isolate. He usually had only one friend at a time. He tended to pick peers in crisis, focusing on their lives instead of his own. He continued this pattern when he became romantically involved, marrying a woman who was a practicing alcoholic. She also had three children and had just left a violent, battering, alcoholic man.

PAUL: "I could protect her. It gave me something to focus on. It gave my life meaning. I was comfortable with the fear and the excitement of impending negativity. However, within months of our wedding her drinking was way out of control. I felt like a failure. At the time we married, I was at a low weight; but within months I started eating again."

Paul's marriage was at least as chaotic as his family's home life had been. After their child was born, his wife began having extramarital affairs that he knew about.

"While we were married, I constantly grazed [nonstop picking and eating] *through the painful times of betrayal, feeling worse and worse about myself and the weight. Frequently the only pleasant times in our house were spent planning and preparing meals. But the meals themselves were battlegrounds. So at times I expressed*

my anger by withdrawing from food and meals. Other
times I ate to stuff my anger.

"The eating was also hidden. Besides grazing all day,
I would stock up on soothing things for nighttime and
eat alone while my wife was out."

Paul was beside himself. He lacked the skills and the
self-worth to do anything but accept his lot. Again he was
left feeling that, no matter what he did, it wasn't right. As
always, food was his ally, literally his only friend.

Paul and his wife finally divorced—at her initiation
and his compliance. He got a full-time job working for
a food vending machine company. This was as suicidal
a move as an alcoholic getting a job as a bartender.

"I was driving around with a whole truck full of chips,
candy, and other junk food. My anger and resentment
with work problems or my life came out in the truck.
Now, instead of waking up from a daze in front of the
refrigerator, I was waking up from a daze in the front
seat of my truck, surrounded by candy wrappers."

In time, Paul's ex-wife became sober and suggested
that he try going to Al-Anon.

"What made me take her suggestion was not so much
her recovery in AA as my own pain, powerlessness, and
feelings that I was going insane. I felt very little con-
nection between what I did and what was happening in
my life. I began to realize that being 'nice' would not
bring people who cared about me into my life. But I
didn't know that I had any other choice.

"What I learned through Al-Anon had to do with self-

care. I discovered that I first had to be nice to myself before I could draw people to me who were kind."

Paul was in such pain, and so lonely and confused, that he was willing to listen to what others said—and it seemed okay. Within six months he began to confront his problem with food.

"I could no longer lose weight or control my eating. Twice a doctor had told me that I was in danger of bringing on diabetes because of my obesity. He said I had to lose weight. I realized that I was killing myself with food, and I knew that that was insane.

"So with the three catalysts—Al-Anon, which encouraged my self-love enough to make my eating habits appear crazy; the vending route, where the food stealing and bingeing made me realize that I had lost control; and the visits to my doctor, who said clearly that my eating was killing me—I had to find help. I turned to another Twelve Step program: Overeaters Anonymous. This time, no authority figure sent me. I went on my own. It meant I had enough self-esteem to be able to love myself enough to do that."

Through Al-Anon and OA, Paul began to deal with both his overeating and his ACOA issues.

"The first issue in recovery for me was self-care. I gave myself acknowledgments for each step of progress I made—for being abstinent that day; for making it through the day with some sense of serenity. It became important to me to do kind things for myself: feeding myself an attractive meal, taking a long hot bath, walking in the rain or on the beach. It felt like letting the

kid have a place to come out in safety. It also felt like letting the real adult come out in safety while parenting the child.''

Paul also had to deal with the conflicting loyalty issues common to children growing up in dysfunctional families.

''The rule of not talking about 'negative' stuff outside the family made me feel as if I were being disloyal when I first entered OA. I stopped Al-Anon for six months, hoping I could do just one program at a time. But then I started feeling crazy about family and relationship issues again. So I concluded early on that, for proper self-care, I need both programs each week to remain stable. With them both, I can generally tell when I am hiding from life through work, sleep, or whatever.

''It's important for me to realize that my recovery must be my priority. I can no longer allow people-pleasing or parent-pleasing responses to bring me down enough to turn to food again. I need to act on my own behalf on the issues, whether or not my parents understand or support me.''

Paul has found that self-care and self-acceptance mean learning to accept and love his own body, something he was never able to do before.

''The self-care stage involved a lot of body work so that I could learn to love myself with whatever body I had. I would stand naked in front of a mirror, saying that I loved my thighs and my butt, parts of my body I had never liked because that was where I always gained the weight. I learned to take someone shopping with me so

that I'd stop picking out clothes that were too big—I needed help to stop thinking of myself as fat. By including that person, I was also breaking the isolation and secrecy I'd grown up with. Women started noticing me and approaching me, and I began to think that I might be sexually attractive, which was very hard for me to accept at first. It was a completely new way of looking at myself."

Another area Paul realized he needed to work on was honesty and forgiveness. He had spent years hiding his eating and feeling terrible about himself for it.

"I had to learn to avoid grazing while preparing and cleaning up after a meal. Initially I set a time limit on my meals to avoid overeating. Eventually I could become less strict with myself because the honesty and forgiveness had healed so much of my self-loathing.

"I know that when I start slipping back into my old patterns, I never 'get away with it.' Even if the weight doesn't shoot up right away, my sense of honesty is affected, and the emotional and spiritual parts of the disease kick in. That's when the old self-critical, condemning, perfectionist ACOA has to start getting honest again—but gently. At times I tell myself, 'I will not eat, no matter what.' At other times I need to quiet the critical part and say, 'My job is to love my Higher Power. To love Paul. All else is a gift.' "

The next issue Paul had to come to terms with was "normalcy."

"I'd always felt different from other people. I now realize that I have a disease that makes me different. By

accepting the disease, I have actually learned how to be with people, how to express myself in groups more freely, how to initiate relationships and maintain intimacy. I no longer have to hide out to survive. Just because I can't eat like normal people doesn't mean I can't learn the social skills required to work, achieve, exercise, and love like other people.

"I've also learned to deal with the issue of making mistakes. I've learned to acknowledge my mistakes without condemning myself or having to beat myself. Before, when I made a mistake, I became the mistake, and I attacked myself or gave up in despair. I believed that if I couldn't do something perfectly, I wouldn't do it at all."

Adult Children often struggle with perfectionism. It's common to see them trying to do recovery perfectly and, when they realize that's not possible, castigating themselves and even giving up in futility.

"Now I see that I set too rigid a standard for myself. I'm just setting myself up to fail. If I think that I can control all of my food issues once and for all and never slip again or get sloppy about my eating habits, then I lose the part of the process that is mine—the footwork in the present."

Paul is recognizing the concept of "staying in the here and now" in recovery. He knows he has to take responsibility for himself in the present and not project into the future or obsess on the past.

Because recovery with food addiction cannot be the "all or nothing" approach that recovery from chemical dependency demands, the struggle over doing recovery "right" is even more difficult for people with an eating disorder. Once they learn that even if they're less than perfect, they're still okay, then they'll be able to live with less fear and a greater willingness to include others in their ongoing recovery.

"My current issue is trust. It's taken seven years in recovery to make it a focused process. I have to trust that I can have an answer that may not always work the way I want it to, but that this is all right. I have other options. I can ask for feedback from others. I can look for help from my Higher Power. The decision is still up to me. I can make a choice about abstinence and live with the outcome. And if it doesn't work, I can decide to change what I'm doing instead of giving up."

Both Al-Anon and OA have played an important part in Paul's recovery.

"I've not been able to do this with just one program. However, with two it's easier to find a balance with my shifting compulsions. Now I can maintain my recovery day to day, rather than switching to a new compulsion.
"As a child, my parents were unable to give me the love and support I needed. So I intellectualized and ate my feelings away. In recovery I have learned to value myself and my feelings. I've learned to choose people in my life who enjoy and love that balance.
"Now, instead of avoiding risk taking or doing whatever others tell me to do, I've learned to trust my decisions about my life and my judgment on how much risk taking is safe.
"Sometimes I have to pretend that everyone I love is dead in order to decide what is best for me or what I want.

*At other times I think of myself as my own child so I can
balance my nurturing for myself with what I give to others.
These trusting, loving skills show up in how I'm dealing
with food, because food mirrors my feelings. This is one
way my Higher Power helps me learn balance.*

*"The trust seems to lead to hope. While I don't know
what is next in recovery, I trust my path and the Higher
Power that is unrolling it before me. And I trust me."*

FELICIA
Age: 41
Compulsive overeater, bulimic
Occupation: Account executive
Recovery Process: AA, therapy

Felicia's eating patterns continued through college.
Shortly after high school she went to business school
and moved out of her parents' home.

*FELICIA: "My roommate—an anorexic nursing stu-
dent—and I had an apartment. We ate toast with
mounds of butter and cinnamon sugar, and then we'd
starve ourselves. I'd binge and sneak peanut butter, ice
cream, and cookies. I'd often steal food out of the refrigerator at night, hoping she wouldn't notice."*

Felicia's primary choice of binge food has always
been ice cream and cookies—the foods her mother offered her sister but not her, and her father's favorite
binge foods as well. Alcohol also became more and

more important in Felicia's life. For her, drinking was synonymous with eating.

But drinking had brought a twist to Felicia's eating disorder. When she began to drink regularly, as a senior in high school, she also frequently became sick and would throw up. She quickly discovered that, after the initial distaste, she felt relieved.

"After I'd thrown up a few times, I found that if I drank enough, I could just get rid of it by vomiting. I'd just go do it and then use mouthwash—I learned early on how to keep my clothes clean during it. I'd discovered a new secret. It didn't take me long to realize that I didn't have to drink to throw up. Vomiting was also the answer to my chronic overeating. I could be totally out of control with eating, yet control my weight the entire time."

Although many compulsive overeaters have been secretly purging for generations, Felicia's purging took place before bulimia had the public recognition it has today.

Compulsive eaters experience powerlessness and a sense of being out of control, but purging restores some sense of control. Unfortunately this only helps to keep the eating disorder hidden and never dealt with. Not only is this psychologically dangerous, it can also be life-threatening if repeated vomiting ruptures the esophagus or the stomach and causes hemorrhaging.

Felicia saw herself as obese when in reality she was not. Most of the time she was generally twenty pounds heavier than the perceived norm. Occasionally this would climb to thirty to forty pounds over the norm. But whatever her weight might be, her relationship to food was always unhealthy. Her use of food had prevented her from learning a healthy way of expressing her feelings. In fact, it had created greater isolation and the need for secrecy in her life. It gave her a false sense of nurturance and satisfaction. And it fed her already existing shame. But when she became bulimic as well, she pushed all of these problems into overdrive.

This is when Felicia became engaged to Jack. She starved herself down to the thinnest she had ever been as an adult. And she moved back home for a month until they were married.

"I was a bundle of nerves while I was staying with my parents. By this point I was sneaking food, starving myself, drinking alcohol nightly, and doing something else I never told anyone about—wetting the bed. I was such a wreck that the doctor prescribed Valium. I was loaded when I got married, but I was thin."

In her marriage Felicia was seeking to fulfill the social aspirations of her socioeconomic background. She had found a well-educated husband; she worked and took night classes at a community college; she partied to show life was fun, and she became a mother.

Food was still the central dynamic in Felicia's life. However, after she got married, she and her husband also began a pattern of drinking every night. As is common with so many people with eating disorders, alcohol became addictive for Felicia as well.

"Food and wine were interchangeable for me. Instead of eating late at night, we'd have a few drinks. We got into gourmet cooking and wine tasting. Then I became pregnant, which was a great excuse to eat.

"I always felt fat and was always trying to lose weight. My husband didn't say much about it, but I knew he dis-

approved just by his looks. He would also buy me clothes that were too small. My mother had always bought me clothes too big for me. No one ever bought clothes for the real me. They bought clothes for their fantasy of me.

"After the birth of our second child it took me a long time to lose the weight that I had gained. My husband backed off from me sexually. He said I was rigid, too uptight, not playful or sensuous.

"He plugged right into my fears that I wasn't enough as a woman, as a wife, as a sexual partner. What hurt the most was that part of me knew that he was right. In reaction, I did what I knew best when I hurt: I ate and I drank and I threw up. I ate and I drank and I threw up. I felt crazy and depressed. I began to realize that I'd lost any of the control over food or alcohol that I'd once had. That scared me.

"As our marriage fell apart, I was devastated. The model I'd learned from my parents was that you dealt with pain by using alcohol. I'd never felt this much pain before because I'd never been allowed to feel. Alcohol, at least temporarily, killed the pain. Alcohol became my friend. I was lonely and scared, and I couldn't turn to my family. They had always told me whenever I cried that I was being silly or shouldn't feel that way. And now my worst fear— that I wasn't really enough—had come true. My marriage was ending, and I felt like a failure."

Felicia and her husband separated. She went back to work part-time and finished her degree in business administration. But her patterns of binge drinking and binge eating also continued. The pressures of school, the divorce, and taking care of two small children made her let go of some of her perfectionism, but Felicia still felt that she just wasn't "enough," as if there weren't enough of her to go around. And, in reality, there wasn't. Felicia had become Superwoman. To nurture herself, she ate and drank, drank and ate.

For reasons she didn't understand, Felicia took a course on alcoholism, even though it wasn't a part of her requirements for school.

"In the class, we had to write about an addiction. I picked food. At this point I went to Overeaters Anonymous and lost fifteen pounds the first two months, but I was anxious and as close to going over the edge as I'd ever been. I was on overload, out of control. OA was working only in terms of weight loss. But once again someone else was controlling my food—my sponsor."

Felicia was using her sponsor the only way she knew. She perceived her sponsor as an authority figure, as the critical, judgmental mother with whom she'd been in a lifelong power struggle. A sponsor is a member of a Twelve Step program that you choose to be your mentor, guide, confidante. He or she is a person you share problems and successes with, who can offer feedback or guidance if you share honestly. Until Felicia dealt more fully with her underlying problems, specifically her anger toward her mother, she would continue to have difficulty using a sponsor. Her Adult Child issues were clearly interfering with her getting the most out of a self-help program.

Felicia was having problems letting go and accepting a Higher Power. Because she felt her drinking was "under control," she didn't tell her OA sponsor about it. She had allowed herself a glimpse of her eating addiction, but her denial was greater toward her alcoholism.

Before long she found that she could not address her eating addiction without first addressing her alcoholism.

Interestingly, while Skip began to lose weight before discovering he had an alcohol problem, most food-addicted alcoholics need to stop their dependence upon alcohol and drugs before they can adequately address the eating disorder.

But Felicia's tolerance for alcohol dropped. What she was learning in her alcoholism class made her face up to what was happening in her own body.

"I had been able to write off or rationalize away all sorts of early- and middle-stage symptoms of my alcoholism. But a drop in tolerance meant my liver wasn't working.

"Then we had to write a paper on a female alcoholic and discuss our feelings. I was overwhelmed with feelings. The next thing I knew, I was in the kitchen with a carton of ice cream and a bottle of Kahlúa liqueur. I looked at them—the food and the alcohol—and I began to cry hysterically. I called a friend who'd been sober for nine months and asked her, 'How do you know if you're really an alcoholic?' I was at an AA meeting the next morning."

Although her recovery had begun, Felicia still had to deal with the old feelings that were a part of her ACOA upbringing.

"Taking on the label 'alcoholic' brought with it a lot of shame. I felt as if I'd failed once again. As I started to deal with how lonely I was and how empty I was, I was so overwhelmed with pain that I turned back to food.

"I had never lost the food obsession. I had never let

go of my mother's critical messages about me and food. I had not surrendered. I had made people, not God, my Higher Power. I began to binge again.

"By the end of year one of sobriety in AA, I had come a long way. I was less anxious, less critical of me and of others, more able to attend to my children, and doing better in school. However, my new drug of choice— actually an old one revived—was clearly sugar."

Felicia's weight had gone up to 180 pounds, and she turned to therapy in order to deal with the bingeing.

"In therapy I began to address my drive for perfection and my negativism. In AA I had included food as a part of my daily meditation, my daily writings, and of my daily inventory. My AA sponsor and I worked the steps for this food addiction. Yet I had never told anyone about the purging—which I continued to do."

People often find that they can attend several kinds of self-help meetings. In Felicia's case OA, AA, ACOA, and Al-Anon would all be appropriate. As many people do, she combined her food and alcohol addictions and attempted to work on both, predominantly in AA. Although this may work for some, it's most likely to be successful only when alcohol is the first drug to be abused. On the other hand, trying to work on both addictions at once can also feed one's denial—primarily the denial regarding food issues.

That is exactly what occurred for Felicia. She was now sober, she knew she had Adult Child issues, she felt a great deal of shame about her body and eating patterns—yet she was still hanging on to control. Not all the truth had been acknowledged or spoken. So, as much as she was making a stab at recovery for her eating disorder, Felicia was still trying to control her own program. She was discriminating what she would and would not be honest about rather than surrendering and being totally honest. She was still externally focused, hoping outside entities would provide control against her overeating.

"Aside from periodic OA meetings and using AA to attend to my eating disorder, I also sought out a nutritionist at times, and an exercise coach. But I remained inconsistent with healthy eating and exercising. I would still binge and purge (not yet telling anyone I did so), I still hated my body and was preoccupied with what others thought. I still felt I needed others to control my eating. Yet this still led to my rebelling when they or I put limits on me around food. I still felt defective, a failure. I still couldn't look in a mirror."

Felicia was a bright, successful career woman who had been in touch with all the appropriate resources for over five years—OA, therapy, and AA. But AA was the only consistent resource in her life. And not surprisingly, recovery from alcoholism was the area in her life where she was having continuous success. She was alcohol and drug free. She was more connected with healthy support people. Her self-esteem was growing, and she was experiencing some joy in her life.

Finally, after five years of sobriety, Felicia's denial cracked. Her controlling behavior, her manipulation of people, places, and things, were out of control. She began to have flashbacks about the childhood incest, and she knew she must seek therapy.

"When I began therapy, my analyst had me do some 'body' work. It meant first seeing my body. All of my life I had avoided mirrors. If I passed anything that showed a reflection, I'd be so anxious I'd nearly have a panic attack. My experience with incest had affected everything that had to do with my body and all that I had done to it. When I looked in a mirror I saw my grandfather."

In dealing with her shame and anger over the incest, Felicia uncovered a lot of rage. As she has grown more and more in touch with the rage, she has been able to release the blocked energy, to release the shame. The more she remembers, the more she is able to parent her inner child who never received the nurturing she needed and deserved.

But Felicia's anger, shame, and need for control—and her struggle with powerlessness—was not related to the sexual molestation alone. It was also connected with her parental relationship. Felicia found that she couldn't deal with one area without tapping into the other. She also discovered that, until then, she had been controlling her Adult Child therapy.

Once the incest was recognized, once Felicia began to release her feelings safely, her sense of shame lessened and she found greater self-acceptance. This empowered her to address other sources of anger and to see clearly how her anger had fueled her eating addiction.

"I knew I had to get angry, but I couldn't. I was bound to my powerlessness."

Felicia had taken a very depressive stance in life. She had used both food and alcohol to provide solace and to anesthetize the pain.

"I was angry at my mother for controlling me. I was angry at her criticism and her perfectionism that had so warped my values. I was angry at her for trying to make me a copy of her. Angry at her for treating me differently from my sister. Angry at her for not listening! Angry at her for not making me special! For not protecting me! For robbing me of self!"

Felicia's recovery is still ongoing. After grief work around the incest, her mother became her focus, because the loss in that relationship was more blatant than the loss of her father. It's easier to identify a loss when it's tangible: Mom did this! And she did that! The loss of her dad was more subtle because it came from what he didn't do.

As many ACOAs do, Felicia found it necessary to address only the issues that felt safe. Food had been the most blatant issue, so she began recovery in OA. But it was in AA that she really felt at home. Her alcohol issues were the safest place for surrender to the recovery process. But food, especially sugar, had been her best friend all her life. The deep and emotionally charged issues underlying her eating disorder would need time, patience, and courage to uncover. It took over five years of active recovery from alcoholism before the incest could and would present itself. And it was only after she began to address the incest that she was totally prepared to deal with her issues with food.

After a year of working with the incest experiences in therapy—with continuing involvement in AA—Felicia found that she could be much more consistent in abstaining from sugar. And after not purging for six months, she was finally able to talk openly about it.

"I am much more loving to myself around food now. I've really done some incredible work—with God's help—in learning to love at least most of my body. I am much less critical of myself than I used to be. Today, I can look in the mirror and enjoy it. I'm like my own teenaged daughter—forever looking in the mirror. My body now has sensations I've never felt before. I was always so busy controlling and discounting, I never even knew I was in pain because I could never feel. I missed over forty years of internal sensations. I was constantly focused on the external—the image, the goal, other people's approval and attention. Now I have my body back. I have me back."

At last Felicia could begin to recognize how much she had neglected her femininity.

"For the first time I have come to recognize that I had experienced masculine power as abusive. Today I'm re-framing that to see the positive aspects of both masculine and feminine power. I see masculine power as competitiveness, as the ability to set limits, to focus on self as well as others, to get results. I see feminine power as softness, creativity, receptivity. I see it as beingness, as process. I want to have access to all sides of me. I particularly need to work on the feminine side—to be more in touch with my intuitions and internal signals. I want to trust me. Up to now, food, alcohol, and my ever-vigilant control had squashed all of that.

"I had rejected and abused my physical being. Today I can look at myself and like what I see. I buy pretty clothes, softer clothes, clothes with color. I nurture my body with exercise, massage, and healthy food. With

*my friends in self-help groups, my sponsor, my thera-
pist, my Higher Power, I believe for the first time in my
life that not only will I be okay, I am okay just as I
am.''*

Recovery Considerations

PRIMARY ADDICTION

Although Adult Child issues are clearly connected with
eating addictions, the compulsive eating that results in
obesity, bulimia, or anorexia needs to be accepted as a
primary addiction. People with eating disorders need to
become involved in a program specializing in eating
addiction. It may be a self-help group of Overeaters
Anonymous, a psychotherapist who specializes in eating addictions, or an outpatient or inpatient eating addiction program.

Eating disorders are abusive to the body, and it is
helpful to begin with a total assessment of your health
to determine a baseline against which you can measure
your ongoing physical recovery. Therefore it is important that those with an eating addiction receive a physical examination by a specialist in eating disorders. It
is necessary to discover whether there are any physiological causes for the obesity. Then the physical consequences of the addiction need to be diagnosed and
treated. Once a commitment is made to follow through
on such a program, it is possible to pursue Adult Child
issues. I have not found it helpful to put a specific time
frame around the period that people are in food addiction recovery before they begin Adult Child work. Once
a commitment is made to an eating addiction program,
I believe one should begin Adult Child work on the
issues around one's relationship with food.

MULTIPLE ADDICTIONS

Addictive personalities often have more than one addiction. As you saw in this chapter, Felicia had an eating addiction and was also chemically dependent, Skip became alcoholic after he began recovery for his eating disorder. Many recovering alcoholics discover in sobriety that they are food-addicted. Food and alcohol often work in a close partnership—either they are abused simultaneously, or one is used to discourage overindulgence in the other.

It's easy to begin to feel overwhelmed when you have to respond to more than one active recovery program. The most important thing to understand up front is that having more than one addiction is quite normal for people with eating and chemical dependencies. Each one needs to be addressed as primary. Do not try to substitute one recovery program for another. The next thing on the agenda is to pay attention to how Adult Child issues contribute to the addiction and/or influence recovery.

It's very common to compare one's recovery rate from one addiction with one's recovery from another addiction. Because there are many similarities in the process of recovery, people often negate the differences. Personally, I would hesitate to say that recovery from one addiction may be easier than another. Recovery from any addiction is different from person to person—and it is always miraculous. Although much progress has been made with understanding alcoholism and drug dependency as diseases, the public still tends to perceive eating disorders as willful behavior. They are not. In addition, there is a significant difference between recovery from eating disorders and other addictions, particularly alcohol and drug addictions.

For chemically dependent people, abstinence from alcohol and mood-altering drugs is the core of recovery. But critical to the understanding of eating disorders is that those with food problems cannot abstain from eating. One must eat to live. This fact creates an incredible difference for the food-addictive person.

When people recover from chemical dependency they learn to live their lives without using any alcohol or drugs to compensate for emotional states. On the other hand, the food-addicted person must learn to live by adjusting to degrees of use of the very thing they're addicted to—food. It's very difficult to regulate the intake of any addictive substance. Food addicts, whether anorexics, bulimics, or overeaters, must rethink what food means to them and then apply that understanding to their lives. They know that compulsive eating and compulsive starving cause them to think, feel, and act in a manner different from "normal," just as chemically dependent people know that drinking or drugging medicates and anesthetizes feelings. While chemically dependent people can stop all alcohol and drug usage, overeaters must deal with food several times a day. This is a difficult challenge, but recovery is possible, as demonstrated in the lives of these four people.

SHAME

People with eating disorders feel such incredible shame. Often the eating addiction see-saws between compensating for the shame and creating the shame. It can become a downward spiral. You must remember that there are deep-seated reasons for the disorder, and that there are people who will both understand this and be of help. You are not a bad person now, and you have never been a bad person. What you have been is scared, lonely, angry, powerless. One of the most important gifts you can give yourself is the opportunity to meet others who are recovering from eating addictions. They will understand and not judge. And they can offer direction and hope.

INCEST

If the need to control, starve, purge, or overeat is in any way connected with a response to incest or sexual molestation, the sexual abuse must be addressed specifically. Incest is prevalent in our society, and an eating disorder is a common response. Whatever the experience, believe me, you were not at fault, and you are not a bad person. You don't need to punish or purge yourself any longer.

FEELINGS

Those with eating addictions are extremely disconnected from their emotional selves. Most Adult Children struggle with learning to identify and express their feelings. They struggle with fears of what will occur should they show their feelings. But the emotional self of the person with an eating disorder is directly linked to this disorder.

In the process of recovery from food addiction, one must experience emotional recovery. Overeating, starving, and purging are defenses erected to protect one from further hurt and pain. Unfortunately, these defenses don't work. Using food to manage feelings may temporarily distort one's perception of the truth, but it cannot alter the truth. Feelings may be disguised, denied, and rationalized, but a painful feeling will not go away until it has run its natural course. Adult Children must talk about their fears of what will occur when they learn to identify their feelings and express them.

Anger is the feeling most repressed in eating addictions. In recovery it is vital to begin to understand that feelings are signals and cues. Feelings are there to help us, to befriend us—not to hurt us. Feelings will not make us go crazy. They can be particularly painful when they're stored away or denied for many years. But it is possible to walk through the pain.

Be open to the fact that you have many repressed feelings, and that you have legitimate things to be angry about. Anger is a natural reaction when one has been hurt. Personally, I don't think it is possible to be raised in a family affected by as much incredible loss as the ones we've been discussing and not be angry. Some Adult Children have more reasons to be angry than others, but all have some anger that needs to be acknowledged to allow for a more complete recovery.

You must face your anger about things that happened to you in the past. Acknowledging anger will not take away all of the hurt, but it does cleanse one's emotional wounds and initiate healing. Once you acknowledge your anger at the past, you will be able to experience the whole rich range of feelings in the present. The anger you might feel at the current experience will become clearer, not clouded by anger and issues from the past. Not being able to identify and display anger is the same as denying it.

As we address how our feelings are connected with food, we can begin to recover from the compulsive eating, the starving, and the purging.

CONTROL

For bulimics and anorexics, seeking control is the central issue. Obesity is more representative of being out of control. The Adult Child must develop healthy concepts about power and control. We often attempt to control people, places, and things—for example, through the image we present to others—or we control our bodies to mask shame or to compensate for incredible feelings of powerlessness. As adults there are choices available to us that we didn't have as children. Any sense of powerlessness we may feel now is often self-imposed.

It will be important to explore what control and power meant when we were children. Without that exploration, a key connection to what overeating, purging, or starving means to us now will be missed. Usually the grief work in that area is necessary. After that, putting the past behind us will be vital to recognizing and accepting where our power lies today.

ISOLATION

Those with eating addictions have often lived isolated from others. Do not isolate yourself during recovery. Isolation leads to loneliness, to controlling behavior, and to greater shame. You deserve better.

Because eating disorders are so much diseases of isolation and control, I believe that it is paramount that one begins the group process quickly in recovery. You are not the only person with this problem, and the faster you realize that, the faster your shame will lessen. A group experience can sound so frightening, but the sooner you try it the better. This is one case where I find that plunging in can be particularly useful. It can be of great help in learning to relinquish the tight control you've maintained over every aspect of your life.

PERFECTIONISM

There is no perfect recovery. People who are compulsive perfectionists were usually raised in families where parental figures had unrealistic expectations of them. As children they internalized those expectations, and today they continue to operate on unrealistic expectations.

When they were children, they needed to do things right—"right" meaning no mistakes—in order to lessen their fears of abandonment and to get approval. As adults these people continue to attempt to be perfect. This is often reflected in their image of the perfect body. They struggle with self-hate and disgust at not matching their perfect image. And they take it out on themselves in their overeating, anorexia, or bulimia. Until we can come to terms with our common humanity, it is likely that many of us will continue to overeat, starve, and purge.

In recovery, the source of this perfectionism needs to be dealt with so that you can come to terms with the fact that you are enough, that you are of value, that you are special, that you are important. We are all vulnerable. We all make mistakes. That's how we learn.

Today I don't eat compulsively, nor do I deprive myself. Most important, I am able to do that without living in fear of myself.

—Compulsive Overeater, Adult Child

Notes

1. L. Drozd, "A Sense of Self Model for the Treatment of (Female) Children of Alcoholics." (Ph.D. diss. California School of Professional Psychology, San Diego, 1986).

3

Moving On
in Recovery

I wrote *Double Duty* out of my conviction that no one should have to go through life with the shame that is created in dysfunctional families. It is my belief that once we are able to understand the dynamics of our Adult Child issues, we can truly begin to work through them. In the life stories you have just read, you've seen how people have chosen various means of working through their issues. It is possible for each and every one of us to have recovery. We no longer have to live our lives based in fear.

The process of recovery allows us to put the negative influences of our past behind us and take responsibility for how we live our life today. It is a process that takes time, patience, and persistence. To put our past behind us, we must come out of denial and begin to speak the truth about our life experiences. We can no longer minimize, rationalize, or discount what really happened to us. We must own our experiences.

The Stages and Steps of Recovery

People tend to move through five distinct stages in the process of Adult Child recovery. The stages presented are a synthesis from the works of Julie Bowden and Herb Gravitz, authors of *Guide to Recovery*.

FIRST STAGE: SURVIVORSHIP

We begin by knowing that we can and will survive. While Adult Children deserve to feel good about their survivorship, they also deserve more in life.

SECOND STAGE: EMERGENT AWARENESS

This is where we recognize that there was something wrong in our childhood and we no longer deny it. We are free to acknowledge our experience and its effects on us. This is often an exhilarating stage—a time in which we feel a sense of direction and hope.

THIRD STAGE: ADDRESSING CORE ISSUES

Once Adult Children have accepted the influence of the past on their lives, they are ready to confront the core issues that have plagued them as adults. It is in this stage that the Adult Child is most apt to need the assistance of others to work through such issues as control; identifying and expressing feelings; needs; limit setting and establishing boundaries; and self-validation. Throughout the entire process the Adult Child is working on trust and shame.

FOURTH STAGE: TRANSFORMATION

This is a time of personal change, of putting into effect the things we've been learning, of risking new behaviors. Transformation leads to internal integration. The work on previous stages has helped us to trust our internal wisdom, and we are now in the process of discarding hurtful beliefs and replacing them with beliefs that nurture loving self-acceptance and self-care.

FIFTH STAGE: GENESIS

Although this is different for each person, Genesis generally involves a new openness to the spiritual aspects of life. This is when we begin to participate in the creation of our own world—not grandiosely, but realistically. Genesis marks the true beginning of our lives as expressed through our unique relationship to the rest of the universe.

As part of the process of working through these recovery stages, I have identified four steps that need to be repeated, often more than once, with each and every issue one is addressing. The four steps are:

- Explore the past
- Connect the past with the present
- Challenge the belief messages
- Learn new skills

EXPLORE THE PAST

Much of the initial process of recovery involves talking about the past. Many people find this both exciting and scary, but the purpose of talking about the past is to put it behind us. This is not meant to be a blaming process; it is the process of speaking your own emotional truth. You talk about the past to undo denial.

This is very important because it is often the first time in our lives that we have been able to talk openly about our experiences. Talking without fear of being rejected or punished allows us to release deep feelings that we have kept inside and that remain hurtful to us. When we do this with others who are participating in the same process, we receive validation for ourselves when we were young.

Most Adult Children have a skewed sense of what "normal" is. Only by talking about our experiences can we put them in a context that helps us recognize our needs and learn how to set appropriate limits and boundaries. More important, we are able to discard the messages that we aren't good enough or that we are inadequate. We begin to feel that we are of real value.

The grieving process is the most emotionally painful part of recovery. It can take months. At times Adult Children have been criticized for focusing on the past too much or for "staying in the problem," as opposed to searching for a solution. However, at this point we are in the process of owning our childhood experiences, and this takes a great deal of time. We don't remember everything all at one time, nor do all of our feelings come to the surface at once.

Adult Children need to own their fears, sadness, hurt, and anger. You don't necessarily want to do that with your parents, but you will want to do it with a counselor, other recovering Adult Children, or a trusted friend. We need to feel safe to be able to trust and to share our vulnerabilities. That can take time.

When we are exploring the past we are doing our "grief work," we are speaking of the losses in our lives. Because the pain of these losses has not been acknowledged or validated, taking the time to grieve for ourselves is important. Left unexamined, these feelings of loss grow into emotional time bombs that can become extremely hurtful if they have no appropriate avenues for expression. We act them out in depression, addictions, compulsive behaviors, hurtful relationships, difficulties with parenting, and so on. It is important that one ultimately moves beyond this first step. If not, you will become stuck in the process and it will become a blaming process, not a grief process.

CONNECT THE PAST WITH THE PRESENT

Another important step in recovery is that of connecting our past with our present. Here, the process focuses on insights. This is where we need to ask ourselves, "How does the past connect with who I am today?" Then we follow this with more and more specific questions.

"How does the fact that I spent so much time in isolation and in a fantasy world as a child affect me today?"

"How does the fact that I was so fearful of making a mistake in my childhood affect me today in my work?"

"How does the fact that I lived with so much fear as a child affect me in personal relationships today?"

We need to ask how our many feelings and behaviors in childhood and adolescence affect who we are today in all the many aspects of our lives, our self-esteem, our work, and our relationships. This allows us to focus more on the present.

CHALLENGE THE BELIEF MESSAGES

Early in the process of exploring the past, we also begin to challenge the childhood beliefs we internalized from our parents. These are beliefs that we heard verbally or experienced behaviorally. Often the messages we internalized were parental "shoulds." "You shouldn't trust others.'' ''You shouldn't be angry.'' ''You shouldn't cry.'' So we need to go back and identify those internalized messages or life scripts. We need to ask ourselves whether those messages are helpful or hurtful, positive or negative. We need to question whether or nor we want to continue to take these internalized messages with us throughout our adulthood.

Helpful messages would be:

All people deserve respect.
People are trustworthy.
You are of value.
It's okay to say No.

Hurtful messages we often heard were:

You can't trust anybody.
No one's going to be there for you.
You can't do anything about it, so don't bother.
Your needs are not important.

It's okay to keep the helpful messages. By acknowledging the ones we're going to keep, we take present-day ownership of them. They no longer belong just to our parents, they are ours as well.

The hurtful messages need to be discarded. This is often done in a symbolic form. For each message tossed out, you will need to create a new helpful one in its place. This is active recovery—you are taking responsibility for how you live your life.

LEARN NEW SKILLS
As we're reading, listening, and sharing, we're also taking another step. We're learning new skills. Much of

recovery involves learning the skills we didn't get the chance to acquire in childhood. These are often such basics as:

Identifying feelings
Expressing feelings
Asking for help
Recognizing options
Problem-solving
Negotiating
Setting limits
Saying No
Saying Yes
Drawing attention to yourself in a positive way
Playing
Relaxing
Listening
Making a decision

Once we learn to use these skills, we're ready to live our lives differently. Now we have choices that haven't been there up to now.

With the healing that results from these four steps, Adult Children will free themselves from viewing life through the lens of addiction. Recovery leads to establishing a balance in life. While life will always pose certain restrictions and problems, the Adult Child now has a range of skills and the awareness of self to cope with and respond to the imperfections that come with life. Recovering does not mean you will never feel pain again, it doesn't guarantee good decisions nor prevent relationship break-ups. It won't necessarily give you the material things you desire. It will offer you an emotional freedom from the past, so that the past no longer dictates your self-worth and esteem. It will give you options; it empowers; it brings you into the "here and now."

In order to take these four steps, we need a continuous flow of information and support. Until the last few years we haven't had the information necessary even to understand what has been going on in our lives.

Recovery Literature

By reading books that support recovery, by attending lectures and workshops, and by becoming part of self-help groups or being in therapy, we can develop the language we need to begin talking about our experiences. We are people who spent our childhood years in sick families where people did not speak the truth and did not acknowledge what was occurring around them. We have so rigidly adhered to the "Don't talk," "Don't feel," "Don't think," "Don't ask questions" rules that, as adults, we really don't have the words or the understanding we need to describe our own experiences of the past or the present. Many Adult Children cannot discern one feeling from another. In addition, we often lack the ability to distinguish the normal from the abnormal.

Reading is often a good place to begin. It is a wonderful adjunct to both therapy and self-help recovery. It will familiarize you with the language that has become common to the recovery movement. More importantly, it will offer you a better understanding of what has happened in your life. Reading will allow your frozen feelings to thaw, and you will begin to realize that you don't have to continue your life with fear, shame, or other hurtful behaviors. Reading will show you that there is a path, a direction, out of the maze. It will help you realize that you are not alone.

As you read, you will begin to see yourself, and you will be amazed. It's as if the author had been raised in your home or had been living side by side with you in your adult life. Nearly every other Adult Child has felt as you have felt: guilty, ashamed, frightened, alone, sad, so unique. Reading helps to lessen that.

But be open to going beyond self-learning and insight. Allowing yourself access to others in recovery is wonderfully validating. It is also freeing to share your issues in the safety of rooms where so many others will identify with you.

Self-Help Groups

In general, self-help groups have been extremely valuable to thousands of people with various maladies. Adult Children have found support, validation, and direction in recovery through Al-Anon, Adult Children of Alcoholics, and Co-Dependents Anonymous. Although most Adult Children who mention participating in self-help groups are usually referring to the Twelve Step process, as you read this book you will see that others found self-help groups in different ways.

In coming together with other Adult Children in self-help groups, you will learn more about what all Adult Children have in common. Participants talk about their struggles and successes while developing problem-solving skills. They also find comfort in the fact that they are not unique, not alone in their problems. Most often the participants come to regard the group as a healthy extended family.

Whatever path you choose, remember, it is important to give self-help groups a fair chance before you say, "That's not for me." Try out different meetings. In Twelve Step meetings the group will often recommend that the newcomer try at least six meetings before making a decision about further participation.

It is common for Adult Children to want to work out problems on their own, to keep their feelings stuffed and controlled. We learned to master that approach a long time ago. But now we need to recognize that our old ways aren't working for us any longer. We need to keep an open mind. The simple act of sharing with another person who has had similar feelings and has encountered similar situations brings us out of denial and isolation. This kind of sharing also offers us a greater awareness of ourselves and a feeling of greater connectedness with others. Often a group experience allows us to accomplish together what we cannot do alone. This is true of both self-help and therapy groups.

Therapy

There are many different types of therapy. Many Adult Children have already spent considerable time in therapy long before they discovered they were ACOAs. It is important to choose a path of recovery that feels safe to you. If you have found therapy to be valuable in the past, then it is likely to be even more helpful now that you are exploring this new information. It is possible that if you seek a therapist who gives credence to Adult Child issues, your experience will be much richer and more beneficial.

The types of therapy available differ, depending on whether the therapists work with people individually or in groups. Some therapies focus on the here and now, dealing with a specific problem; others are more process-oriented. Some are conducted for a specific period of time with all participants having the same goals; others are more long term, with or without a closing date. Here, the participants all have similar backgrounds and similar goals, yet work on issues specific to themselves.

Should you want to talk to someone about the fact that you are an Adult Child, and discuss specific issues, I recommend that you begin in one of two places. First, ask other Adult Children you know if they are in therapy and whom they see. Ask them what they are getting out of therapy. What do they like and what do they not like about this specific therapist and the process? Acquire the names of two or three therapists and make an appointment with each one for an exploratory session. This is your time to ask the therapist questions, to decide if this is the right person to guide and support you in your recovery process. Some people can make this evaluation in a short telephone conversation; others require a face-to-face interview. The important thing is to find a therapist who feels right for you and then to allow yourself to make a commitment to the therapeutic process.

The second way to get a therapist is by calling an information and referral service knowledgeable about chemical dependency resources. This is most often the local council on alcoholism and a chemical dependency treatment program.

Crucial to your recovery is that your counselor or therapist understand the process of chemical dependency and Adult Child issues. In the exploratory sessions you can ask if they have done any reading in these areas. Have they taken specific training in this field? If the therapist discounts or minimizes addiction or ACOA issues, consider moving on to someone willing to address such issues in your therapy. You do not need to be with a therapist who works only with Adult Children. However, you do need someone sensitive to what being an ACOA means, someone knowledgeable about the dynamics of being raised in a chemically dependent home and the effects these have on your adult life.

Pacing Yourself

Although the timing of the issues to be addressed in the process of recovery may be different for the Dual Identity Adult Child who has a primary addiction, the process is similar.

Because of the intensification of effects experienced by those who are DD/DI, it is important that you not judge the pace at which you respond to a recovery program or compare your recovery rate with other people's. Often, the beginning weeks and months of recovery are the most difficult for DD/DI Adult Children because of their greater fear of giving up control and of trusting, along with their experiencing greater denial and, certainly, greater shame. Although you will walk through the same process as others, you may need to take more time to do so. All recovery is taken in steps, not leaps and bounds. But sometimes the DD/DI person may need to take baby steps.

In addition, you will also need to address the dynamics of the added trauma in your life—physical abuse and/or sexual abuse. After recognizing the similarities among Adult Children and addressing the issues common to all, DD/DI ACOAs will need to retrace their steps: explore the past, connect with the present, and challenge the shoulds as they relate to their DD/DI. These first three stages tend to take a longer period of time, but once they've been explored, "learning new skills" comes as readily to the DD/DI as to any Adult Child.

While I've said it many times in *Double Duty,* I would like to offer this advice one more time. If you don't feel safe in a group process, you may find that individual therapy offers you an added safety net. For those who participate in Twelve Step programs, the concept of individual sponsorship is highly beneficial. While there are many rewards in the group experience, if you don't feel comfortable with it, simply allow your self-awareness to direct you to what is most appropriate for fulfilling your present needs. Your recovery deserves to be safe. Be patient with yourself.

Resistances

The two greatest resistances to recovery are first, wanting the process to be pain free, and second, wanting to do it all by ourselves.

Adult Children often want recovery, but they'd like it without the pain. That's understandable. It's not been safe previously to feel; we feel out of control and bad for being emotional. And should we begin to get in touch with our feelings, we often feel years and years of pain, which seems overwhelming. But we *must walk through the pain* in order to put it behind us. Today we have the inner strength and can do it! As vulnerable as we feel, nothing bad has to happen to us. And that is certainly true when we allow others to be a part of our process—which puts us in contact with the second resistance—wanting to do recovery in isolation.

When we are frightened, we can easily fall back into our old pattern of solitary self-reliance. Now is the time to remind ourselves of the price we pay for isolation. It is my belief that, even if we could do recovery by ourselves, we deserve so much more. For far too long we have lived in isolation—if not social, then certainly emotional isolation. We deserve to give ourselves the rich experience of allowing others to be a part of our process. There are thousands of Adult Children in recovery today who would be willing to offer you support through both self-help and therapy groups. There are increasing numbers of educators, counselors, and therapists who are skilled in walking Adult Children through recovery. Other people can help make recovery a much easier and, very often, a much safer process.

A Word of Caution

Adult Children have a tendency to want to make decisions when they are in the midst of their feelings: "I feel sad, therefore I must score." "I am angry, therefore I will score." While feelings are cues and signals about our needs, it is important to not make any major life changes in early recovery.

At that point it is easy to find fault with much of how we live our lives. We tell ourselves: "I never would have chosen this partner ten years ago if I hadn't been so sick, so I must get out of this relationship." "My job is as sick as the family I was raised in. I want to change careers." "I need to be that child I was never allowed to be, so I'm going to walk away from my marriage and children and recapture my childhood."

Although your relationship and your job may have problems, or you want to go back to your childhood, making abrupt decisions in early recovery rarely leads to the dream scenario you have hoped for. Early recovery may bring many feelings and insights, but you haven't yet integrated the new skills that will enable you to live your life differently. When we make a change just "to make changes," we often end up re-creating a situation identical with the one we are escaping. Even more important, there is a tendency in early recovery to project feelings from our childhood onto present-day situations.

With time, such projections lessen, and what seemed so bad is not nearly the crisis it first appeared to be. As you develop new skills, you will have the opportunity to act differently in your current relationships, at work, and with friends. At this later stage the decisions you make will be based more on choice. You may still choose to make certain changes, but they will be based more on your present-day perspective, more on the strong foundation of your ongoing recovery.

Love and Loyalty

While we can get very excited about recovery, telling the truth about our past often makes us feel disloyal to our families. After all, we love our parents. This is when we need to remember that being in recovery doesn't mean we don't love our parents. Most of us do. Often we have loved them against all odds, and that is why our hurts are so deep.

In recovery we aren't betraying those parts of our parents that truly loved us. Healthy parents love their children and want them to live free, happy lives. They don't want us to carry pain, fear, anguish, or loneliness with us. They want us to feel good about who we are. At this point in recovery the most important disloyalty to guard against is disloyalty to ourselves for not allowing ourselves a new way of life.

If your parents have continued to deteriorate in their disease, your new behavior will alter the nature of your relationship. Even if your parents have experienced recovery, your relationship may still need to be redefined. That can hurt. But whether or not your parents are in recovery, *you* can have recovery. And you can maintain a relationship with them if you choose. This relationship will have limitations—but the old relationship had limitations, too.

You may be wondering how many of your feelings and perceptions, if any, you might be able to share with your parents. Personally, I would not recommend that you share much of your experience with your parents in the early months of recovery. After that, what you share, how much you share, with whom and when, are important questions that need a great deal of thought. Generally speaking, we don't want to keep recovery a secret. At the same time, if our parents have remained sick, they will most likely respond hurtfully to any information we give them.

If you are thinking of talking directly to your parents about your recovery, consider approaching each parent separately. Then ask yourself: "What do I want to tell him (her)?" "Why do I want to say this?" "Will it help me if I say it?" "Am I saying it to hurt them?" "What do I hope will happen?" "How realistic are my expectations?" It is important to think ahead about what it is you want to disclose. "Living our recovery" as we relate to our parents is an even greater goal than sharing all of our feelings and thoughts with them.

The Reward for Going Deeper

So many feelings will awaken as you read this book and reflect on your own experiences. Please let me remind you again that, when you have bottled up your feelings for so long, it is easy to feel that you are losing control when they begin to well up. In the beginning we can feel overwhelmed by our emotions. Sometimes we don't even know what they are or why we are having them. Don't be critical of yourself at this time. The fact that you are feeling is significant. Adult Children frequently have many feelings at one time. Often you may not know the exact source of the feeling as you experience it. Sometimes we only know what we feel after the fact. But if you keep talking, in time the source will connect with the feeling. Practice identifying your feelings and gradually experiment with telling someone about them.

As you move through recovery, ask yourself periodically which feelings are the easiest for you to show people and which are more difficult. What fears have you about showing the more difficult feelings? If you are frightened of showing your anger or sadness, ask yourself what you fear will happen if you show that feeling. Tell someone about the fears. Are your fears based on your present experience, or are they from your childhood? So often we have fears left over from long-ago experiences, but until we question them we don't realize it. Now ask yourself what you need to do to be able to express those feelings. Then give it a try.

The recovery process is often described as peeling an onion—below one layer there is another and then another. Looking at DD/DI issues brings us one layer closer to the core. When you work intensely on a particular area, there may be a deep pain associated with certain feelings for a period of time. Then there will be periods where your recovery enjoys smooth sailing. But again, unexpectedly, you will find yourself confronting another serious and painful issue. Remember: you haven't done anything wrong, you just couldn't have reached this layer of recovery before you addressed the other layers. Sometimes the reward for going deeper is going deeper. With each layer of recovery you are a step closer to resolving old issues and letting go of the past.

Strategies to Help with the Pitfalls

We all have particular pitfalls in recovery, but they aren't necessarily unique to us. There are clues common to many of us that can be used as signals to warn ourselves that we are slipping back into old behaviors or attitudes. It will be helpful for you to identify yours and to know what you need to do when you recognize them.

Take a minute right now to finish the following sentence in at least four different ways.

"I know I'm in trouble when I _____."
"I know I'm in trouble when I _____."
"I know I'm in trouble when I _____."
"I know I'm in trouble when I _____."

So often I've heard people say, "I know I am in trouble when . . .

* * *

I isolate myself.''
I minimize my feelings.''
I start critical self-talk again.''
I get overinvolved in such areas as work or fixing
    others.''
I feel inadequate or inferior.''
I don't want to trust anybody.''

We can begin to avoid these potholes if we know
what to look for. But we also need to plan out what
we're going to do if we find ourselves there. So take
your specific pitfalls and develop a strategy plan for
each one.

Isolate. Have a list of phone numbers of people to call.
Tell them of my behavior. Identify my most recent feelings or talk about what was occurring at the time I
began to separate from my feelings.

Minimizing Feelings. What am I really feeling? What
message am I sending myself right now that is making
me stuff this feeling? I'm going to challenge that message because I know it's an old message from the past.
What is it I've been learning lately about healthy feelings?

Critical self-talk. Stop!! Quit projecting. Recognize that
I'm into "all or nothing" thinking again. What is it I'm
feeling right this minute? Keep telling myself, "It's okay
to make a mistake.''

Overinvolvement. What am I avoiding? What am I run-
ning away from? Whose approval am I seeking?

* * *

Feeling Inadequate. I'm going to make an effort to spend time with recovering friends. I'm going to pay attention to my daily victories. I'll praise myself for them. I'll give myself healthy rewards.

Not Trusting Anybody. I recognize that the issue is "all or nothing." Whom do I trust now? What is it I trust about that person? What little things do I trust with other people?

Now you will have a list of warning signs and a set of new behaviors that you can act on to counteract those old attitudes and messages. Planning ahead makes it easier for you to respond in a healthy manner when the time comes. And those times will come. We are human. Many of us are recovering from terrifying childhoods. All of us are recovering from close to twenty years, if not more, of hurtful messages and coping skills that no longer work for us.

Recovery is a step-by-step process. It is hard work. It is exciting work. It can be emotionally painful at times. It can be confusing at times. But, ultimately, recovery is validating and extremely rewarding.

The *Next* Step

As recovering Adult Children, one of the things we learn about ourselves is that we are people of courage and strength. When we were children we had the courage and strength to endure. However we responded to the pain in our lives, it was our way of surviving. We found our lifelines and used them well.

But today, in recovery, we find that we often need to give up those defenses. This can be very difficult—for they have been our major form of protection. Yet, one by one, we find we have the courage to do just that. It is not possible to read Double Duty/Dual Identity life stories and not see the magnitude of pain induced without also recognizing the inner strength that guides us to seek out and travel the path to recovery that helps us to overcome the pain.

Recovery comes for the Double Duty/Dual Identity person as we embrace all of our being.

Our body.

Our culture.

Our vulnerability.

Our strengths—which we developed in response to the multiple issues we had to deal with in our lives.

While the following manifesto has relevance for us all, I created it for, dedicate, and offer it to those who have struggled so long and so bravely with Double Duties and Dual Identities.

Double Duty/Dual Identity Manifesto

- I take responsibililty for how I live my life. I no longer walk through life hiding behind masks for self protection.
- I no longer live a life based on fear and shame.
- I reject messages of shame, whether they come from others or through my own critical self-talk. I create affirming messages of love and empowerment.
- I am willing to ask for help. I am willing and able to include others in my process.

- I no longer accept a life of loneliness. Now I feel secure when I am alone, and comfort when I am with others.
- I am of value, and this remains true no matter what mistakes I might make.
- I trust in myself, and I trust in others.
- I no longer live in fear of being abandoned. I trust in my own value even when I feel the most vulnerable.
- I identify and establish healthy boundaries so I will not be violated, emotionally or physically. I am learning the skills I need to set the limits that maintain those boundaries.
- I identify and seek recovery from my compulsions, addictions, and self-defeating behaviors.
- I recognize I have choices and am willing to act on those choices. At the same time, I also recognize where my power lies.
- I take pride in my heritage. I acknowledge and embrace the healthy aspects of my culture.
- I no longer deny and reject parts of my physical being. I accept my body and find the strengths in my disabilities.
- I deserve to live a life unencumbered by sexual stigmas.
- I recognize and honor what is unique about myself and my personal history. I affirm the positives in my differences.
- I speak my truth.
- I recognize and celebrate my strengths.
- I believe in my right to happiness, dignity, and respect.
- I love and accept all of my self.

Appendixes

Anonymous Fellowship Acronyms

Common Acronyms of Twelve-Step Anonymous Fellowships Referred to within *Double Duty*.

AA	Alcoholics Anonymous
ACA	Adult Children of Alcoholics
ACOA	Adult Children of Alcoholics
CODA	Co-Dependents Anonymous
CA	Cocaine Anonymous
GA	Gamblers Anonymous
NA	Narcotics Anonymous
OA	Overeaters Anonymous

Appendix 1
The Twelve Steps of Alcoholics Anonymous

1. We admitted we were powerless over alcohol—that our lives had become unmanageable.
2. Came to believe that a Power greater than ourselves could restore us to sanity.
3. Made a decision to turn our will and our lives over to the care of God *as we understood Him.*
4. Made a searching and fearless moral inventory of ourselves.
5. Admitted to God, to ourselves, and to another human being the exact nature of our wrongs.
6. Were entirely ready to have God remove all these defects of character.
7. Humbly asked Him to remove our shortcomings.
8. Made a list of all persons we had harmed, and became willing to make amends to them all.
9. Made direct amends to such people wherever possible, except when to do so would injure them or others.
10. Continued to take personal inventory and when we were wrong promptly admitted it.
11. Sought through prayer and meditation to improve our conscious contact with God *as we understood Him,* praying only for knowledge of His will for us and the power to carry that out.
12. Having had a spiritual awakening as the result of these Steps, we tried to carry this message to alcoholics, and to practice these principles in all our affairs.

The Twelve Steps reprinted with permission of Alcoholics Anonymous World Services, Inc.

Appendix 2
Are You a Food Addict?

	YES	NO
1. Are you intensely afraid of becoming fat?	___	___
2. Do you feel fat even when others say you are thin or emaciated?	___	___
3. Do you like to shop for food and cook for others but prefer not to eat the meals you make?	___	___
4. Do you have eating rituals (for example, cutting food into tiny bites, eating only certain foods in a certain order at a particular time of day)?	___	___
5. Have you lost 25 percent of your minimum body weight through diets and fasts?	___	___
6. When you feel hungry, do you usually refrain from eating?	___	___
7. If you are a female of childbearing age, have you stopped having menstrual periods?	___	___
8. Do you often experience cold hands and feet, dry skin, or cracked fingernails?	___	___
9. Do you have a covering of fuzzy hair over your body?	___	___
10. Do you often feel depressed, guilty, angry, or inadequate?	___	___

11. When people express concern about your low   __ __
    weight, do you deny that anything is wrong?

12. Do you often exercise strenuously or for long   __ __
    periods of time even when you feel tired or
    sick?

13. Have you ever eaten a large amount of food   __ __
    and then fasted, forced yourself to vomit, or
    used laxatives to purge yourself?

14. Are you frequently on a rigid diet?   __ __

15. Do you regularly experience stomachaches or   __ __
    constipation?

16. Do you eat large quantities of food in a short   __ __
    period of time, usually high-calorie, simple-
    carbohydrate foods that can be easily ingested
    (for example, bread, pasta, cake, cookies, ice
    cream, or mashed potatoes)?

17. Do you eat in secret, hide food, or lie about   __ __
    your eating?

18. Have you ever stolen food or money to buy   __ __
    food so that you could start or continue a
    binge?

19. Do you feel guilt and remorse about your eat-   __ __
    ing behavior?

20. Do you start eating even when you are not   __ __
    hungry?

21. Is it hard for you to stop eating even when you __ __
    want to?

22. Do you eat to escape problems, to relax, or to   __ __
    have fun?

23. After finishing a meal, do you worry about   __ __
    making it to the next meal without getting
    hungry in between?

24. Have others expressed concern about your ob-   __ __
    session with food?

25. Do you worry that your eating behavior is ab-   __ __
    normal?

26. Do you fall asleep after eating?   __ __

27. Do you regularly fast, use laxatives or diet   __ __
    pills, induce vomiting, or exercise excessively
    to avoid gaining weight?

28. Does your weight fluctuate 10 pounds or more   __ __
from alternate bingeing and purging?
29. Are your neck glands swollen?   __ __
30. Do you have scars on the back of your hands   __ __
from forced vomiting?

SCORING: *Five or more "Yes" answers within any of the following three groups of questions strongly suggest the presence of an eating disorder: questions 1–15, anorexia nervosa; questions 14–26, binge eating; questions 12–30, bulimia*

Appendix 3
The Original Laundry List—
Adult Children of Alcoholics

THE PROBLEM
The characteristics we seem to have in common due to our being brought up in an alcoholic household:

A. We became isolated and afraid of people and authority figures.

B. We became approval seekers and lost our identity in the process.

C. We are frightened by angry people and any personal criticism.

D. We either become alcoholics, marry them, or both, or find another compulsive personality such as a workaholic to fulfill our sick abandonment needs.

E. We live life from the viewpoint of victims and are attracted by that weakness in our love and friendship relationships.

F. We have an overdeveloped sense of responsibility and it is easier for us to be concerned with others rather than ourselves; this enables us not to look too closely at our own faults, etc.

G. We get guilt feelings when we stand up for ourselves instead of giving in to others.

H. We became addicted to excitement.

I. We confuse love and pity and tend to "love" people we can "pity" and "rescue."

J. We have stuffed our feelings from our traumatic childhoods and have lost the ability to feel or express our feelings because it hurts so much. (Denial)

K. We judge ourselves harshly and have a very low sense of self-esteem.

L. We are dependent personalities who are terrified of abandonment and will do anything to hold on to a relationship in order not to experience painful abandonment feelings that we received from living with sick people who were never there emotionally for us.

M. Alcoholism is a family disease and we became para-alcoholics and took on the characteristics of that disease even though we did not pick up the drink.

N. Para-alcoholics are reactors rather than actors.

THE SOLUTION

By attending Adult Children of Alcoholics meetings on a regular basis, we learn that we can live our lives in a more meaningful manner; we learn to change our attitudes and old patterns of behavior and habits; to find serenity, even happiness.

A. Alcoholism is a *three-fold disease*: mental, physical, and spiritual; our parents were victims of this disease, which either ends in death or insanity. This is the beginning of the gift of forgiveness.

B. We learn to put the focus on ourselves and to be good to ourselves.

C. We learn to detach with love; tough love.

D. We use the slogans: LET GO, LET GOD; EASY DOES IT; ONE DAY AT A TIME, etc.

E. We learn to feel our feelings, to accept and express them, and to build our self-esteem.

F. Through working the steps, we learn to accept the disease and to realize that our lives have become unmanageable and that we are powerless over the disease and the alcoholic. As we become willing to admit our defects and our sick thinking, we are able to change our attitudes and our reactions into actions. By working the program daily, admitting that we are powerless, we come to believe eventually in the spirituality of the program—that there is a solution other than ourselves, the group, a Higher Power, God as we understand Him, Her or It. By sharing our experiences, relating to others, welcoming newcomers, serving our groups, we build our self-esteem.

G. We learn to love ourselves and in this way we are able to love others in a healthier way.

H. We use telephone therapy with program people who understand us.

I. The serenity prayer is our major prayer.

Appendix 4
Do You Have the Disease of Alcoholism?

Alcoholism strikes one out of every ten people who drink. Not everyone has the physiological makeup to become alcoholic, but anyone who drinks could be at risk. Alcoholism doesn't discriminate. It afflicts people of all ethnic backgrounds, professions, and economic levels. It is not known precisely what causes this disease, but drinking is clearly a prerequisite. Therefore everyone who drinks should periodically evaluate their drinking patterns and behavior. Here is a self-test to help you review the role alcohol plays in your life. These questions incorporate many of the common symptoms of alcoholism. This test is intended to help you determine if you or someone you know needs to find out more about alcoholism; it is not intended to be used to establish the diagnosis of alcholism.

	YES	NO
1. Do you ever drink heavily when you are disappointed, under pressure or have had a quarrel with someone?	___	___
2. Can you handle more alcohol now than when you first started to drink?	___	___

167

3. Have you ever been unable to remember part of the previous evening, even though your friends say you didn't pass out? __ __

4. When drinking with other people, do you try to have a few extra drinks when others won't know about it? __ __

5. Do you sometimes feel uncomfortable if alcohol is not available? __ __

6. Are you in more of a hurry to get your first drink of the day than you used to be? __ __

7. Do you sometimes feel a little guilty about your drinking? __ __

8. Has a family member or close friend ever expressed concern or complained about your drinking? __ __

9. Have you been having more memory "blackouts" recently? __ __

10. Do you often want to continue drinking after your friends say they have had enough? __ __

11. Do you usually have a reason for the occasions when you drink heavily? __ __

12. When you are sober, do you often regret things you have done or said while you were drinking? __ __

13. Have you ever switched brands or drinks following different plans to control your drinking? __ __

14. Have you sometimes failed to keep the promises you have made to yourself about controlling or cutting down on your drinking? __ __

15. Have you ever had a DWI (driving while intoxicated) or DUI (driving under the influence of alcohol) violation, or any other legal problem related to your drinking? __ __

16. Do you try to avoid family or close friends while you are drinking? __ __

17. Are you having more financial, work, school and/or family problems as a result of your drinking? __ __

18. Has your physician ever advised you to cut down on your drinking? __ __

19. Do you eat very little or irregularly during the periods when you are drinking? __ __

20. Do you sometimes have the "shakes" in the   __ __
    morning and find that it helps to have a "lit-
    tle" drink, tranquilizer or medication of some
    kind?
21. Have you recently noticed that you cannot   __ __
    drink as much as you once did?
22. Do you sometimes stay drunk for several days __ __
    at a time?
23. After periods of drinking do you sometimes   __ __
    see or hear things that aren't there?
24. Have you ever gone to anyone for help about   __ __
    your drinking?
25. Do you ever feel depressed or anxious before, __ __
    during or after periods of heavy drinking?
26. Have any of your blood relatives ever had a   __ __
    problem with alcohol?

*Any "Yes" answer indicates a probable symptom of alcohol-
ism. "Yes" answers to several of the questions indicate the
following stages of alcoholism:*

   Questions 1 to 8: Early stage.
   Questions 9 to 21: Middle stage.
   Questions 22 to 26: Beginning of final stage.

Appendix 5
Professional Resources

Anorexia Nervosa and Related Eating Disorders (ANRED)
P.O. Box 5102
Eugene, Oregon 97405
(503)344-1144

Cocaine Hotline (800)662-HELP

Children of Alcoholics Foundation (CAF)
200 Park Avenue, 31st Floor
New York, NY 10166
(212)351-2680

Institute on Black Chemical Abuse (IBCA)
2614 Nicollet Avenue South
Minneapolis, MN 55408
(612)871-7878

National Asian Pacific Families Against Substance Abuse (NAPAFASA)
6303 Friendship Court
Bethesda, MD 20817
(301)530-0945

National Association of Anorexia Nervosa and Associated Disorders (ANAD)
P.O. Box 7
Highland Park, IL 60611
(708)831-3438

National Association of Children of Alcoholics NACOA)
31582 Coast Highway
Suite B
South Laguna Beach, CA 92677
(714)499-3889

National Association of Lesbian and Gay Alcoholism Professionals (NALGAP)
204 West 20th Street
New York, NY 10011
(212)713-5074

National Black Alcoholism Council (NBAC)
417 South Dearborn Street, Suite 1000
Chicago, IL 60605
(312)663-5780

National Coalition Against Domestic Violence
1500 Massachusetts Avenue, NW, Suite 35
Washington, DC 20005
(202)638-6388

National Coalition of Hispanic Health and Human Services Organization (COSSMHO)
1030 15th Street NW, St. 1053
Washington, DC 20005
(202)371-2100

National Hispanic Family Against Drug Abuse (NHFADA)
1511 K Street, Suite 1029
Washington, DC 20005
(202)393-5136

Native American Association for Children of Alcoholics (NANACOA)
P.O. Box 18736
Seattle, WA 98118

Parents United
AMACU Coordinator
P.O. Box 952
San Jose, CA 95108
(408)453-7611, ext. 150
Treatment oriented

Phobia Society of America
133 Rollins Avenue, Suite 4B
Rockville, MD 20852
(301)231-9350

Victims of Incest Can Emerge Survivors in Action (VOICES)
Voices in Action, Inc.
P.O. Box 148309
Chicago, Il 60614
(312)327-1500

Appendix 6
Self-Help Groups Based on the Twelve Step Program of AA

ACOA Intergroup of Greater New York, Inc.
P.O. Box 363
Murray Hill Station
New York, NY 10016-0363
(212)582-0840

Adult Children of Alcoholics (ACA)
2225 Sepulveda Blvd., #200
Torrance, CA 90505
(213)534-1815

Al-Anon Family Groups
P.O. Box 862
Midtown Station
New York, NY 10018-0862
(212)302-7240

Alateen
Al-Anon Family Groups
P.O. Box 862

Midtown Station
New York, NY 10018-0862
(212)302-7240

Alcoholics Anonymous (AA)
Box 459
Grand Central Station
New York, NY 10163
(212)686-1100

Anorexics / Bulimics Anonymous (ABA)
P.O. Box 112214
San Diego, CA 92111
(619)273-3108

Batterers Anonymous (BA)
BA Press
1269 NE Street
San Bernardino, CA 92405
(714)884-6809

Cocaine Anonymous (CA)
6125 Washington Blvd., Suite
  202
Los Angeles, CA 90230
(213)559-5833

Co-Dependents Anonymous
  (CODA)
P.O. Box 5508
Glendale, AZ 85312-5508
(602)979-1751

Gamblers Anonymous (GA)
National Service Office
P.O. Box 17173
Los Angeles, CA 90017
(213)386-8789

Narcotics Anonymous (NA)
World Services Office
16155 Wyandotte Street
Van Nuys, CA 91406
(818)780-3951

Overeaters Anonymous (OA)
World Services Office
4025 Spencer Street, Suite
  203
Torrance, CA 90503
(213)542-8363

Parents Anonymous (PA)
6733 South Sepulveda Blvd.
Los Angeles, CA 90045
(213)410-9732
(800)421-0353

Sex Addicts Anonymous
  (SAA)
Box 3038
Minneapolis, MN 55403
(612)339-0217

Sexaholics Anonymous (SA)
P.O. Box 300
Simi Valley, CA 93062
(805)584-3235

Sex and Love Addicts Anon-
  ymous (SLAA)
(The Augustine Fellowship)
P.O. Box 119
New Town Branch
Boston, MA 02258
(617)332-1845

Survivors of Incest Anonymous (SIA)
P.O. Box 21817
Baltimore, MD 21222
(301) 282-3400

Women for Sobriety
Box 618
Quakertown, PA 18951
(215)536-8026

Bibliography

EATING DISORDERS

Hampshire, Elizabeth. *Freedom from Food*. Park Ridge, Ill.: Parkside Publishers, 1987.

Hollis, Judi. *Fat Is a Family Affair*. New York: Harper & Row, 1988.

Orbach, Susie. *Fat Is a Feminist Issue: The Anti-Diet Guide to Permanent Weight Loss*. New York: Berkley Publishing Group, 1987.

Roth, Geneen. *Breaking Free From Compulsive Eating*. New York: New American Library, 1985.

———.*Feeding the Hungry Heart*. New York: New American Library, 1982.

———.*Why Weight? A Guide to Ending Compulsive Eating*. New York: New American Library, 1989.

———.*When Food is Love*. New York: Dutton, 1991.

SEXUAL ABUSE

Bass, Ellen, and Laura Davis. *The Courage to Heal: A Guide for Women Survivors of Child Sexual Abuse*. New York: Harper & Row, 1988.

Blume, E. Sue. *Secret Survivors: Uncovering Incest and Its Aftereffects in Women*. New York: John Wiley & Sons, 1990.

Davis, Laura. *The Courage to Heal Workbook*. New York: Harper & Row, 1988.

Engel, Beverly. *The Right to Innocence*. New York: Fawcett, 1989.

Gil, Eliana. *Outgrowing the Pain*. New York: Dell, 1988.

Lew, Michael. *Victims No Longer*. New York: Harper & Row, 1990.

ADULT CHILDREN AND CO-DEPENDENTS

Ackerman, Robert. *Growing in the Shadow*. Deerfield Beach, Fla.: Health Communications, Inc., 1986.

———. *Let Go & Grow: Recovery for Adult Children*. Deerfield Beach, Fla.: Health Communications, Inc., 1987.

———. *Same House, Different Home*. Deerfield Beach, Fla.: Health Communications, Inc., 1987.

Beattie, Melody. *Beyond Codependency: And Getting Better All the Time*. Center City, Minn.: Hazelden Publishing, 1989.

———. *Codependent No More: How to Stop Controlling and Start Caring for Yourself*. New York: Harper & Row, 1988.

Black, Claudia. *"It Will Never Happen to Me."* New York: Ballantine Books, 1987.

———. *"My Dad Loves Me, My Dad Has a Disease."* Denver, Colo.: MAC Pub., 1979.

———. *Repeat After Me*. Denver, Colo.: MAC Pub., 1985.

Bradshaw, John. *Bradshaw on the Family: A Revolutionary Way of Self-Discovery*. Deerfield Beach, Fla.: Health Communications, Inc., 1988.

———. *Homecoming: Reclaiming and Championing Your Inner Child*. New York: Bantam, 1990.

Cermak, Timmen L. *Time to Heal: The Road to Recovery for Adult Children of Alcoholics*. Los Angeles: Jeremy P. Tarcher, Inc., 1988.

Fossum, Merle A., and Marilyn J. Mason. *Facing Shame: Families in Recovery*. New York: W. W. Norton & Co., 1986.

Gravitz, Herbert L., and Julie D. Bowden. *Guide to Recovery: A Book for Adult Children of Alcoholics*. Holmes Beach, Fla.: Learning Publications, Inc., 1986.

Greenleaf, Jael. *Co-Alcoholic, Para-Alcoholic: Who's Who and What's the Difference*. Denver, Colo.: MAC Pub., 1987.

Halvorson, Ronald S., and Valerie B. Deilgat, eds., with "Friends in Recovery" staff. *Twelve Steps—A Way Out: A Working Guide for Adult Children of Alcoholics and Other Dysfunctional Families*. San Diego, Calif.: Recovery Publications, 1987.

Kritsberg, Wayne. *The ACOA Syndrome*. Deerfield Beach, Fla.: Health Communications, Inc., 1985.

Middelton-Moz, Jane, and Lorie Dwinell. *After the Tears.* Deerfield Beach, Fla.: Health Communications, Inc., 1986.

Norwood, Robin. *Women Who Love Too Much.* New York: Pocket Books, 1986.

O'Gorman, Patricia, and Phil Oliver Diaz. *Self-Parenting.* Deerfield Beach, Fla.: Health Communications, Inc., 1988.

Robinson, Bryan E. *Working with Children of Alcoholics.* Lexington, Mass.: Lexington Books, 1989.

Sanford, Linda. *Strong at the Broken Places.* New York: Random House, 1990.

Smith, Ann. *Grandchildren of Alcoholics.* Deerfield Beach, Fla.: Health Communications, Inc., 1988.

Striano, Judi. *How to Find a Good Psychotherapist: A Consumer Guide.* Santa Barbara, Calif.: Professional Press, 1987.

Subby, Robert. *Lost in the Shuffle.* Deerfield Beach, Fla.: Health Communications, Inc., 1987.

Wegscheider-Cruse, Sharon. *Choicemaking.* Deerfield Beach, Fla.: Health Communications, Inc., 1985.

Whitfield, Charles L. *Healing the Child Within.* Deerfield Beach, Fla.: Health Communications, Inc., 1987.

Woititz, Janet G. *Adult Children of Alcoholics.* Deerfield Beach, Florida: Health Communications, Inc., 1983.

———. *Healing Your Sexual Self.* Deerfield Beach, Fla.: Health Communications, Inc., 1989.

———. *Struggle for Intimacy.* Deerfield Beach, Fla.: Health Communications, Inc., 1985.

RELATIONSHIPS

Covington, Stephanie, and Liana Beckett. *Leaving the Enchanted Forest.* New York: Harper & Row, 1988.

Cruse, Joe. *Painful Affairs.* Deerfield Beach, Fla.: Health Communications, Inc., 1988.

Lerner, Harriet G. *Dance of Anger: A Woman's Guide to Changing the Patterns of Intimate Relationships.* New York: Harper & Row, 1986.

Wegscheider-Cruse, Sharon. *Coupleship: How to Have a Relationship.* Deerfield Beach, Fla.: Health Communications, Inc., 1988.

INSPIRATIONAL

Black, Claudia. *"It's Never Too Late to Have a Happy Childhood."* New York: Ballantine Books, 1989.

Lerner, Rokelle. *Daily Affirmations*. Deerfield Beach, Fla.: Health Communications, Inc., 1985.

Somers, Suzanne. *Keeping Secrets*. New York: Warner Books, 1988.

Wegscheider-Cruse, Sharon. *Miracle of Recovery*. Deerfield Beach, Fla.: Health Communications, Inc., 1989.

Index

SOBERING INSIGHT FOR THE ALCOHOLIC . . . AND THE LOVED ONES WHO WANT TO HELP THEM